THE
PROSTITUTION
TRAP

First published in 1997 by
Gary Allen Pty Ltd
9, Cooper St
Smithfield
NSW 2164

Priesley, Sarah, 1970-
The Prostitution Trap

ISBN 1 875169 68 7

1.Priesley, Sarah, 1970-. 2. Prostitutes - Australia-
Biography. I. Title.

306.742092

Printed in Australia by
Robertson Printing
352 Ferntree Gully Rd
Notting Hill 3149

Designed, typeset and produced in Australia for
Gary Allen Pty Ltd by
Allan Cornwell Pty Ltd,
25, Churchill Rd,
Mt Martha,
VIC 3934.

THE PROSTITUTION TRAP

Sarah Priesley

Gary Allen Pty Ltd, 9 Cooper St Smithfield, NSW 2164

To working girls everywhere

Acknowledgements

Writing this book made me never want to go back to prostitution ever again. I'd like to thank the friends who were there for me, whether or not they were aware of it, when I'd given up. Many thanks to Tina, who gave me the peace to write and never thought I was wasting my time. Thanks to Erica, who lent me her understanding ear, when I needed someone to confide in. Thanks to the surfers next door, who made interesting scenery. Thanks to the people from AWARD for instilling some faith in my ability, and giving me some direction. Special thanks to my grandmother, whose kindness I will always be grateful for. Thanks to Katrina for being a good friend. Thanks to Alex, who encouraged me to keep writing and many thanks to my publisher, Gary Allen, for publishing my book.

List Of Contents

Chapter 1

Change

As I boarded the bus to take me to Gatwick airport from my small English country town, I hugged my mother goodbye, and realised it would be a long time before I'd see her again. I felt sad, hurt, confused, and lost, but I was sure I was doing the right thing.

The last few years at home had been hell and I no longer felt safe living in a house that my older, abusive drug-addicted brother filled with hate and violence. I'd been so unhappy, although leaving my mum behind to sufffer him by herself made me feel guilty. But the tensions had built up and I no longer felt like sticking around to take it. For about two years now, he'd been working away from home and when he had no work he'd come back home, bringing his problems and smack habit with him. Drunk or high on drugs, he'd explode into rages whenever he felt like it. No-one had any control over him and it was hard to make him stop.

I was nineteen, and I'd applied for a working visa for one year in Australia, an escape route from home, to leave my troubled family behind and have a chance of some fun. I'd read loads of library books about Australia and it seemed that no matter where you turned it was sun, sand and holiday time. I had bought my ticket straight away, a return, but I had no intention of going back.

I didn't just want to go on a holiday for a year and then come back and have to face the same problems all over again. Running away and escaping the whole nightmare seemed a much better solution — an excuse to start over again somewhere else in the world. I'd dreamt up a whole new future that I thought would somehow reveal itself to me.

It was a long flight, and by the time I got into Sydney I was exhausted. As I stepped outside into the brilliant sunshine I realised I was completely over-dressed in woolly jumper, jacket and long skirt. Since I'd left for Australia in such a hurry, I had nowhere to stay, nor did I have any nice relatives or friends to flag me down at the airport, so I caught a taxi to one of the inner-city hotels.

As the taxi wound its way down the freeway from the airport, the realization of actually being in Australia all of a sudden dawned on me. Everything had happened so quickly. I'd been so excited and eager to get here, I'd hardly thought things through properly.

I'd heard plenty of stories from friends and teachers about Australia and read books about the country, so I had some idea of what it was going to be like. Leaving behind everyday life and travelling around the world had always appealed to the adventurous side of my nature, but I didn't in reality feel secure enough to take off just like that. A girl I knew, whose family had been trying to emigrate to Australia for years, had told me all about the different visas I could apply for and the idea of working in an English speaking country that I was familiar with for a year appealed to me.

I remember the day after my visa came through, I booked my ticket for practically the next day, without really thinking about it or talking it through with my mum. My brother was working away at the time and I just wanted to disappear, so I wouldn't have to see him ever again. He'd been getting steadily worse and more dangerous. He kept a shotgun in his room and mum had tried to take it away from him, but he wouldn't let her. I thought that sooner or later he might use it on us. He was taking a lot of drugs and he was up and down all the time. I was sure he was capable of anything. Mum had filed a court order against him to keep him away, but that never seemed to stop him, he'd just break in and the police would lock him up for a night and then he'd be back again. It was as if we were constantly holding our breath to see what he would do next. It felt like we were being terrorised. Both mum and I were scared and I hated the fact that I couldn't defend myself or my mother against him.

But now I was actually in Australia I felt different. I felt that everything would fall into place.

I was a novice in the Australian way but I felt quite proud that I had made the journey over. I tipped the porter something like five cents, without realising, for bringing my suitcases to the room. I drifted into a fretful sleep, and woke up to the sound of children splashing in the pool outside.

I had come to Australia with very little money as I had borrowed almost everything but the fare on Visa. To the Australian Embassy it would have looked as if I had money on paper, but in reality I had only enough for a few more days at this hotel. I hadn't worked out the currency so I wasn't even sure how much it was really costing me.

I wandered outside towards the bus-stop, basking in the late afternoon sun, and caught a bus into the city centre. Looking out the window, I was trying to see where everyone was as the driver wound down to Sydney Harbour, which seemed like an interesting place to get off. In London I was used to hundreds of people bustling around, but obviously on a Saturday afternoon in Sydney it was quite different. At first I found it a bit unsettling and had a frightening feeling that I had made a mistake. I'd decided before I left England that I would stay in Australia until I got residency, so that I'd never have to go back home and live in England again. But I hadn't realised that Australia would be so quiet. Still, it was only my first impression. One thing I did notice, straight away, was that the people were a lot more relaxed, as I watched everyone walking by Sydney Harbour in all its tourist glory.

I grabbed a paper before heading back to my hotel room to settle down for some more restless sleep and Rage TV.

I was panicking about what I'd be doing for a job. In England I'd mainly done canteen work, then some graveshift factory work thrown in before I left, and before that I'd worked in offices as a receptionist and a junior, but I'd been sacked from all of the office jobs apparently for being dumb.

Since I was used to mundane and boring jobs, and it was what I felt most comfortable with — and really all that I could do — I settled back to circle the lines of kitchen hands wanted. My eyes passed through the columns of masseuses listed on the other page, and I thought that massage would be easy enough, that any one could do it. Yet I felt I wouldn't be attractive enough, so I let it pass.

Getting up early on Monday morning, I checked out of the hotel, which had been great, but since I'd worked out the Australian currency and found it was costing too much I moved to a local hostel instead. My last luxury was to be the taxi I caught to the neighbouring suburb.

The hostel was full of backpackers, everyone with a long tale of their travels. I must have looked like a broke holiday-maker, with my nice suitcase stuffed full of clothes, and I hadn't even one epic tale on me. I was glad of the cheap accommodation since it gave me time to look for a job. I felt homesick and I'd lie on my bunk bed crying in the afternoon, or at night when everyone else was asleep, thinking about crawling back to England with my tail between my legs.

Luckily I got the first kitchen-hand job I applied for, and the boss was glad to take me on, even though I was just on a working visa. Getting a job, and knowing that I wouldn't be living on chocolate bars and salad sandwiches for the next week, brought my mood right up, and I felt I was once again in swinging holiday mode, even though my new job meant getting up at six in the morning.

I started going out at night to the local pubs and bars. At one, the Hard Rock Cafe, I met an American sailor who'd just docked for a few days. I started seeing him, and looked forward to our nightly snogging sessions. Since I had landed in Australia I was finding it hard to get my mind off sex. Kissing never seemed so good, and I was yearning to have his cock inside me.

I'd lost my virginity only just before I left England, with my first boyfriend, Andy. I'd always been interested in sex, from nine or ten years of age, and I'd sit in class daydreaming about boys' penises or touching my friend's developed, naked body. When the teens hit, I'd have crushes on one particular guy in the class, but my shyness and insecurity would stop me from saying anything to them. Then around the summer just before I left England, I started playing around with a few guys, although it never got to the sex bit until I met Andy. I really liked him — he was the dark, brooding type, tall, with a nice body.

We did it in his car, the second night we met .We'd been out for a few drinks at a pub before and he drove me down to a deserted laneway. He was a few years older than me and I remember feeling a bit scared. But by this stage, I'd been aching to try sex —most of my friends had lost their virginity while still at school. He was good-looking and I was easily turned on by his fingers. My pants were soaking wet by the time he slipped them down my legs. He got on top of me and squeezed his cock inside. Eventually the pain gave way to exquisite pleasure, as he went deeper inside me. I couldn't believe I'd waited so long to experience this much fun. We had sex a lot of times after that, in his car, or at his parents' place, until we split up. When he was gone, I missed him: he'd opened the door to sex for me and I loved the pleasure I got from it ... I was intrigued, I suppose, because I'd waited so long.

Although I did have some mixed emotions about sex, I'd had an abused past, which I tried my best to forget. My brother and his friends had sexually abused me from primary school age and there were vague memories of one of my uncles doing the same. At the time I accepted it as normal — I never told anyone — I don't know why, because it made me feel so bad.

The kitchen-hand job wasn't all that it should have been; the chef turned out to be a sleaze on wheels, and I felt very uncomfortable about his following me around with a hard-on. I'd suffered the same groping male bosses in England, and I'd often gone home upset, not telling anyone about it. I never had the courage to tell them to leave me alone.

So I quit the job and slept with the sailor. He took me to an expensive-looking hotel, where they asked for a hundred dollars deposit for the key. The sex wasn't that good; he had a small, skinny-looking cock that he stuck inside me too quickly. He went down to lick my pussy, poking his tongue in and out, and then frantically licking it. After all that he lit a cigarette by the window, and said something about heading back to the barracks.

When I woke up in the morning he'd gone and I was left to hand in the key, for which I got his hundred dollars deposit. It was enough money to get to Queensland, so I bought a ticket to go by coach the next day. Someone had told me that Surfers Paradise was okay and that it was hot all the time. I'd been working on a good suntan, so it seemed like the right place to head for.

Surfers looked built up, like a Spanish resort in a quiet season. It was a nice change from Sydney, which was so spread out; it seemed all the action in Surfers happened in the same place, and I was just in time for Christmas, which was only a week away. This time I stayed in a different kind of hostel, more like a flat, shared between six people. It was bright, clean and apparently the best one they had in Surfers. They had topless bathing in the pool outside, which did seem quite unusual for a hostel — obviously things were a lot more relaxed in Queensland.

I set out in search of another job. It seemed that the best approach in a holiday town was to go around asking at the different cafes. It was a lonely trek from one to the next until I came upon Sumer's Souvlaki, and it seemed I'd struck gold.

Sumer and his business partner appeared to like me straight away. They said I could start next day and I'd be working on a casual basis, cash in hand, when they needed me. It was better than nothing, and I was only paying ten dollars a day at the backpackers' hostel.

I got into a routine of getting up in the morning and sunbaking on the beach, which was only two minutes away from the backpackers' hostel, and then going in to work in the afternoon. It was a far cry from England and its cold weather, and all the problems I'd had back there. I was beginning to relax and enjoy the hot weather, and I wrote a letter to my grandmother saying that I was okay. I'd been in Australia now for a month.

Sumer turned out to be just another sleaze. In fact, he was worse than all my sleazy bosses put together, and I had all his friends to contend with as well, in and out of the kitchen when I'd be washing up and cleaning. It now dawned on me that Sumer might only have hired me because I was young; that he wanted someone to get his cock hard as well as clean his dishes. Usually at the second shift, which I'd work from seven until ten at night, he'd come up behind me while I'd be clearing up the last of the dishes, and he'd push his cock into my backside, while he pretended to be massaging my shoulders. I would keep quiet and just take it because it was easier than having no job. Usually he could tell when I'd had enough, and he'd go and finish himself off in the toilet. I found him so disgusting, but I had no idea how to handle it, so I just let him do it. He would have done it to every young girl who worked there. I felt like telling his wife who used to pop in sometimes, but again that would only have cost me my job.

At night when I got back from work, I'd get ready and go out to nightclubs — it was like being in a candy shop, there were so many cute guys. I met another American and wanted to sleep with him straight away. This one was really cute, and I couldn't wait to fuck him. Unfortunately he couldn't get it up, so instead we smoked a joint and sat in his car eating ice cream and listening to the radio.

Undeterred, on Christmas Eve I met a married English guy who'd been living in Australia for the last ten years. He still had the strong Cockney accent. We went down to the beach after talking for a few hours, and as we sat down I started kissing his neck. He got turned on straight away, and he gently pushed me down on to the sand, then pulled my pants down. He undid his trousers and I reached down to touch him. He was huge. I gasped as he pushed it inside me. It felt so good, and as he fucked me I hazily thought, this is the sex I've been waiting for. I could feel every inch of his huge hard-on as he gently thrust it inside me. It felt so magical, lying on the beach so late at night, tipsy from drinking too much and tasting the salty water on our skin. I closed my eyes and took in the pure pleasure and abandonement of having him inside me, of the thrill of having just met him a few hours ago. And as it was now Christmas Day, it was a good present to myself.

I saw him a few times after that but he was twice my age and we didn't really have much in common, except for our love of sex. Besides, he was married and he had three children, so that was that.

After some serious club searching I met George who was seriously gorgeous. He was Greek and from Canberra. He told me he was modelling part-time, and studying real estate. He was so beautiful. We'd kiss for hours, and push our bodies up against each other on the lawn outside my hostel. We didn't have sex because neither of us made the move to take the other's clothes off, and I was quite happy just lying back and kissing in the night's warm air. Just before he left to go back to Canberra, I arranged to meet him for one last time in the night club where we'd first met. But even though I looked for him all night I couldn't find him.

I had never even got to say goodbye, and I felt that I really liked him. My heart ached for days. I pined for him. Sumer said he understood, and tried to show his compassion one night by pulling his cock out and asking me to understand him. I felt a rush of anger and disgust. I wanted this job and I needed the money, but I didn't want to suck this guy's cock for it. He looked a sorrowful sight standing there, with his cock hanging out, a tired-looking middle-aged man. I wanted to laugh, but I was so furious at him I pushed him aside and ran towards the door. I was totally disgusted at his behaviour, and I was just about to run off when I remembered that he hadn't paid me for the night's work. I needed the money, so I went back to the door, where he handed over thirty dollars.

I ran to the beach in tears and threw myself onto the sand. Once again, I felt totally alone, that no-one could help me. Everything was going wrong; nothing was going my way. I must have been terribly naive to have landed myself in such a sticky situation. The worst thing was that I thought if I felt sorry enough for myself someone would get me out of it, but it just kept getting worse. Back at the hostel I lay in tears on the grass outside. I was an unbelievable mess. Missing George and being accosted by a pervert was just too much.

The next morning I felt better after a long sleep. I had no idea what I was going to do, but I knew jobs were scarce, so I considered going back to Sumer's with my tail between my legs. I knew it would be an awkward situation but I could see a worse one arising if I didn't have any money. He took me back and we both pretended nothing had happened.

Weeks passed, as did the people who came to and left the hostel. I went through one cyclone and three men by the time I was ready to leave. I was beginning to wonder what else would be around the corner, as I moved in to share accommodation with an elderly couple in Leonard Avenue.

They were nice people. She was an artist, he a plumber. It was a small flat but we got along quite well. I told them I was in love with a Canberra boy, that I wanted to stay in Australia and how much I hated England. They seemed to understand and wanted to help.

Work was depressingly quiet after the Christmas rush and Sumer was making the excuse that he couldn't afford to keep me on. He was desperate to sell his business because everything was running at a loss. He'd been trying to sell it for years. I thought that was punishment in itself for his being a disgusting sleaze. I left the job on friendly terms and he even bought me a bottle of whiskey, that slipped through the paper bag he'd brought it in and smashed into pieces on the pavement. I suppose at the time it kind of symbolised both our lives.

Once again I hardly had any money, and it was the last resort when I left my purse at a telephone booth. It contained all the money I had left. Now I was truly at my lowest ebb. I was so distressed I cried non-stop for hours as I watched the rain fall down in buckets from the Queensland sky. I called my mum in England and she seemed surprised to hear from me. She wanted to know that I was okay, and I told her everything was fine. I knew from the tone of her voice that she was nearly crying. I felt bad that I'd left her with only a day's notice to come to a country so far away. But at that time, if I'd stayed home, I probably would have killed myself. I'd been so depressed back home, I'd been pretty close to the edge. Everything had been dragging me down. Mum had noticed and she'd gone into this big speech of how I'd better not try and kill myself. At least being broke in Queensland was better than being dead in England, I consoled myself.

The first place that I looked for a new job was in the local newspapers. Before I even started I knew that I just wanted a simple job with no hassles. As I scanned the columns of local jobs I noticed more ads for masseuses. One said 'No experience necessary', then it had dollar signs written after it.

Working as a masseuse seemed a good idea after all. What could be easier than bending over a guy and giving him a massage? You needed no experience, only zero brain power and a pair of hands. How terribly naive I was.

I called a number and a woman told me to come in for an interview. Innocent as I was I went along down to a place in Bungles Avenue that seemed like a nice, charming little house hidden away under some leafy trees. I buzzed the doorbell and was greeted by a woman in her late forties, with a strong French accent. She wore her blonde hair in a tight bun as older French women do. She told me her name was Nicole and ushered me through the reception area into a waiting-room. She left me there while she went to get me a drink.

I looked around at the couches and chairs, and tables with magazines spread over them. It could have been any waiting-room in any office but the blinds were shut and the lights were dimmed. I became a bit nervous and edgy and I was beginning to wonder what type of place this was. I looked at a framed piece of paper hanging on the wall that said 'Strictly massage only'. That settled my mind until Nicole came back with the drink and asked me whether I knew 'What we do here?' I muttered something like 'Yes, of course', but I wasn't really sure. I just didn't want to look like an idiot.

A few of the girls working there walked past and I noticed they were wearing very short skirts and tight clingy tops that revealed their breasts. They were heavily made-up and one was carrying a bottle of baby oil. Nicole went on to say that I would have to wear something sexy and short since the clients picked the girls from two or three for their massage. The waiting-room was where the girls popped their heads around to say 'Hello', she said, and that's how the guys made their choices. I thought if I were getting a massage I wouldn't fuss so much about what the girl looked like.

It was beginning to appear that these clients wanted more than just a massage. Nicole was not exactly saying much, so I could only presume that having sex on these premises must be illegal, but they did it anyway. What I wasn't sure of was whether I could do just massage. I never got to ask because Nicole was busy with the phone, so I left with her 'Goodbye' and 'I'll see you tonight and don't forget the short skirt'.

As I walked back I tried to talk myself out of it. I wasn't cut out to be a prostitute. Even though the receptionist hadn't made it clear exactly what I would be doing, she'd beaten around the bush enough for me to realise that sex would have to be included as well as a back rub. I thought about trying somewhere else, but maybe all massage places were the same. It had taken me long enough to build up the courage to respond to a massage ad, so I thought I might as well find out what it was all about. Anyway, if I didn't like it I could always leave.

That night I brought along the tight clingy black skirt that Nicole had so adamantly recommended in the interview, and a loose flowery blouse and sandals. I had no high heels or sexy lingerie, but really, I didn't think that mattered at the time. Innocent I was then, but I now realise that all new girls who hadn't worked before were very quick money-makers for the owners, with bonuses for the receptionists.

Once again I rang the door bell and Nicole let me in with a wide smile. She showed me straight through to the changing-room, telling me to get dressed straight away because there were regular clients already waiting. Changing as quickly as I could, I barely looked around at the tiny changing-room with fluorescent lighting and a shower in the corner. After I dressed I checked out my appearance in the full-length mirror. I looked young, vulnerable and very scared.

I walked into the clients' waiting-room where three Chinese men were entertaining themselves with porn magazines. I introduced myself as Samantha — as discussed earlier — and they nodded enthusiastically. One of the cheekier, younger ones beckoned me over to sit on his knee. He was very friendly and wanted to know if it was my first night. I felt very embarrased, but I nodded shyly that it was. He put his hand on my leg and smiled broadly back at me. He wanted to see me in a room and so did his two friends. They were going to wait until he'd finished, they said. It was bizarre, hearing three men talking about my body as if it was a piece of meat, and I felt very uncomfortable as the young Chinese man led me to one of the massage rooms.

I think Peter, as he said his name was, had been here that many times he knew his way around, and was familiar with the routine. He handed me over the hundred dollars, which I took back to Nicole. Now that I was more in the swing of things she was leaking out more information: I would get half of that hundred and any tips he gave me. She handed me a packet of condoms and said she would deduct the cost from my wages. I went back into the room wondering what the hell I was doing here. At this stage I was almost ready to bolt out the door and run down the road back home.

When I got back into the room Peter had arranged the couch that had previously stood up against the wall — by the massage table — into a mattress on the floor with a sheet thrown over it. The lights were dimmed and he was standing there naked. I was not used to seeing a stranger I'd met just two minutes before standing naked before me. Sure, I'd been having casual sex, but not this casual. I didn't want to have sex with him. I wasn't turned on and I was frightened, and I didn't care about the money; I just wanted to leave.

I knew I would feel like an idiot if I turned back now, so I started to take off my blouse; after all I had known all along, hadn't I?

I was playing with the buttons of my blouse as slowly as possible and with an aching feeling in my stomach. I pulled my shirt open and reached behind my back to unhook my bra. I had very small, young-looking breasts that pointed out, with tiny nipples. The client looked at them and I

Change

squirmed in my sandals — I'd always been very conscious
of my small breast size. He seemed to like them and he
asked again how old I was. I told him the truth, that I was
nineteen, but he seemed convinced that I was lying and
that I was really only sixteen.

Unzipping my skirt, I let it fall to the ground as I had
my blouse and bra. I reached down to take my sandals off
and lastly my pants. Feeling very exposed and very, very
naked I sat down on the bed next to Peter, who was waiting
expectantly with a hard cock and a sixty-nine position already in mind. I straddled his body and sucked on his
cock, which tasted of cold flesh and cheap soap. I felt that
I was going through all of the motions of sucking a man's
cock, but it wasn't registering in my brain. As I sucked, I
started to cry softly. Tears spilled onto his balls as he prod-
ded his fingers into my vagina. He didn't seem to notice
anything was wrong and just carried on. Inside myself, I
felt I was dying. Doing this was taking my dignity away
and I couldn't believe that I had sunk this low, to let a
stranger use my body for his pleasure with only money as
recompense. I had reached my lowest ruin; now I was wal-
lowing in it. What would it take to feel worse than this?

The client seemed pleased that I'd sucked his cock with
no condom — I was to find out later it was standard to use
one. He seemed more than eager to fuck me, so I gave
him the condom, which he put on himself, then he climbed
on top of me and stuck his cock inside me. He thrusted a
few times, then came with a gasp, got back off and lay by
my side with a condom full of come. There was blood on
the end of it — the shock of the the whole thing must
have brought on my period — I felt embarrassed, but he

didn't seem to notice as he lay there in a very relaxed state. He wanted to extend the time to another half-hour, which passed in a haze of more cock sucking and thrusting and more blood. At the end of it he got up, had a shower, put his clothes back on, quarrelled with the receptionist about the extension price and went back to his friends.

One of the other working girls, in her late twenties, popped her head around to see how it had gone. She looked at the ruffled sheets and the condom lying on the massage table with blood all over them. She seemed a bit perplexed about the entire thing. I really didn't seem to have much idea about it; I was very naive. She offered me the first piece of advice I was to hear there: stick a piece of dish-washing sponge up yourself, to soak up the blood when you are on your period. That way you can still make money.

Peter's friend wanted to try me next, so I went straight back in the room. Things were moving so quickly I could hardly say no. This client was a lot older and he just wanted some polite conversation and quick sex. The half-hour booking was over in ten minutes and I'd just made another fifty dollars. It seemed that money would be the only compensation now that I had done it, lost my innocence, or some part of my innocence. Why turn back? I was past the point of no return.

After Peter's friend I saw an Australian, and after that I felt quite numb about sex with strangers, but with two hundred dollars in my pocket at the end of the night I felt a lot better. I didn't have to worry where the next dollar was coming from, and as I walked home I talked myself into the idea of just working a few more weeks so I could save some money. Maybe then I could pay someone to be my pretend de facto, if that's what it took to stay in Australia.

Back home the next day I told the artist and the plumber that I was working the late shift at a petrol station. This meant that I could do the very late shift at work, which went until three in the morning, without them getting suspicious.

Going to work as a prostitute just required the same routine as a normal job. You had your shift: the responsibility to get there; the getting ready; the waiting around; it was hardly glamorous or exciting. It was just a quick buck in exchange for time with your body. The only way to stop yourself from getting hurt, I was told, was to distance yourself during the booking. I was beginning to learn it was not a good idea to take anything too personally either.

The girls who worked there were pretty bitchy. Most had worked for more than a year and were a lot older, and no doubt they could have done without competition from a young girl who hadn't worked before. Because I was new, I had clients — mainly Asians — coming in for me all the time. Peter, my first client, had put the word out among the Chinese community that there was a young girl who hadn't worked before. Even though I had been wised up about using a condom for oral, the Asian clients thought I was great because I had really pale skin and tiny breasts, which they loved. The Asians had smaller cocks than the Westerners so it made my job easier anyway.

With the money that I was earning, averaging between one hundred on a bad night and four hundred on a good one, I started furiously saving. I kept on telling everyone that I would work for only a couple of weeks, but they just kept saying I'd get used to the money and I'd keep doing it, as they had. The money was the only reason I was doing it. The girls spent a lot of money on clothes, make-up, partying generally, anything they couldn't afford on an average wage. Some of them were single mothers who needed the money, some had a few drug problems but most just liked the steady flow of quick cash. I just wanted money so that I could save it for later. Everyone wanted it for something.

We were paid on a nightly basis and if you had a good week you could walk out with about one thousand dollars, which made a big difference from the usual ten-dollar-an-hour jobs.

In the first few days of working, because it was still so new to me, I liked the sex at times when the clients were good looking or nice. Some of the regular guys would take their time and really spoil me, by giving me a massage and making me feel more relaxed, so it was less of a job and more of a nice experience. Or they were good in bed, and I loved sex anyway, so at times I thought it was an easy job.

Then a bad client would come along, usually with problems and a bad attitude towards women, and really take it out on me. He'd order me around and grab my body too hard and fuck me for half an hour so hard I could hardly walk.

I had a condom break with such a client, who insisted on fucking me for half an hour from the time I got into the room until the time I left. He was thrusting so hard the rubber tore inside me, and when I put my hand down to see whether the condom was still there I just felt skin and I panicked.

I got up and felt warm come dribble down my thighs. Frantically I mopped it up with tissues and asked whether he was okay, meaning whether he had AIDS. He said, 'Yeah, everything's fine'. I went to the shower and desperately soaped myself down, until I was sure there was no come left inside me. I told myself that everything would be fine, although I was terrified that I'd contracted something and would have to wait three months or more to find out. When I'd finished in the shower, he was still lying there on the mattress, waiting for me to come back.

The room was hot and the sickly smell of his come lingered in the air. He wanted to fuck me again: as he said he still had some time left. I just couldn't believe it.

Normally, a client thought that if you looked clean and you hadn't worked for long, then you couldn't possibly have any diseases. So they wouldn't care and they'd just want to keep going, while you're left panicking about whether you've caught something.

Some clients would pull the condom off before they put their cock inside if you didn't watch them. The girls told me to use lubrication with the condoms, which in the first week of working replaced my natural lubrication with a more processed one. When I started working the late shift until three in the morning, after about five clients, there was no way I could feel any sexual exitement, even if they were cute.

After my twentieth birthday, I was ready to leave. I wanted to go to Canberra and see if I could find George. I still felt I had a place for him in my heart, and I was sure if I saw him again he'd sweep me back into his arms. I knew it was a long shot, but it was better than being a prostitute.

The Prostitution Trap

I vowed to the girls at work that once I was there I'd get a straight job, but they just said I was wasting my time with George and that I'd carry on working.

At the back of my mind common sense asked how could money be an objective, if you are generally unhappy. Most of the time you feel like dirt, after a bad client, or sometimes even a good one. To me it seemed like a vicious circle, a complicated merry-go-round. In a matter of two weeks I decided I wanted to get off that complicated merry-go-round because I couldn't see the point of it in the long term. I really couldn't imagine doing it beyond a desperation for money, and a solution for a cash flow crisis. But all the girls umm-ed and ah-ed and said I'd do it again.

Chapter 2

Where's George?

I had the money for a coach ride to Canberra, and I'd managed to save three thousand dollars just in case I met someone I could pay to help me get my residency.

It was a long bus ride. I'd been brought up with very little money and I'd always seen my mum struggling to pay bills, so it never occurred to me to spend my money on a flight; I was no big spender. But once I got there and checked into a hotel, I became accustomed to just doing nothing. It was nice to wander around the city centre, then head back to the hotel to read or watch television. I didn't worry about getting a job because I had some money saved.

The Prostitution Trap

Besides I was here on a mission: I wanted to find George.
I went out in search of him in night clubs and bars.
Canberra was a quiet city and not many people actually
went out, but I still couldn't find him.

Slowly my savings began to dwindle, even though I was
living quite moderately. I came to the conclusion that I'd
have to work again just to keep my savings up. I'd got
used to the quick, easy money in Queensland and now I
wanted more. I really liked the freedom that working gave
me. I didn't have to answer to anybody and my time was
my own. And there wouldn't be any more sleazy bosses: if
men wanted to touch my body now they had to pay for it.

I looked in the Yellow Pages and decided on A Dab of
Perfume. All the brothels were in the same area and there
were plenty of them. It was apparent that the sex industry
was well and truly legal here in Canberra. I went for an
interview straight away, and a woman dressed in a business suit showed me through a proper licensed brothel
which she owned and ran with her husband. There were
six working-rooms altogether and each was decorated
sumptuously in red, very different from the massage house
I'd worked at before. Here there was a spa, sauna, laundry
facilities, piles and piles of towels, and the girls changing-
room was huge in comparison to the other place.

Suzie, my gracious hostess, was a little concerned at
my lack of working experience, since the sex industry was
hardly for beginners here in the sex capital of Australia.
But as we chatted over orange juice she seemed to think
that I'd do well. She suggested that I bleach my dark brown
hair blonde, since the clients preferred blondes. I liked my
hair natural, so I told her if the clients preferred blondes,

then it was their bad luck.

It seemed that now I was a bona fide prostitute: I'd moved into a different league, and unknowingly set up my future for a number of years. Working for Suzie made me realise how much money you could actually make in the industry. The night I started, I listened intently as the other working girls told me how they'd earned thousands of dollars since they'd started. They all said that I should work for a few years, save some money and then get out — if I could. Surprisingly, most of the girls had boyfriends; some knew that they worked and some didn't. I found it astonishing how prostitution had been part of their life for years.

My first client was a man in his sixties. Before he booked me he wanted to know whether he could lick my pussy. I wasn't used to explicit questions, but I agreed. I took him to one of the rooms and he handed me a hundred dollars for half an hour. Before I left the room he winked at me, and said I was young enough to be his daughter.

I took the money to Suzie who was at the front desk, and then went to the changing-room to get the condoms and lubrication. I looked in the mirror to brush my hair: I had worn more make-up than usual, and I was wearing a black dress that was body-hugging, with no bra so my nipples showed through. I went to the wash-basin, hitched up my dress, pulled down my pants and wiped my cunt clean with soap and tissues. I was sure the last thing my client wanted to taste was my latest visit to the toilet.

He was eagerly waiting in the room, naked on the bed. He beckoned me over and I sat next to him, stroking his penis. I took my clothes off and lay down on the bed with my legs apart. He crouched down between my legs, letting his tongue move over my cunt. I closed my eyes and enjoyed the sensation of his warm tongue moving on me, even though he was over sixty. I'd had my first orgasm in Queensland when I first started working. It blew my mind that sex was actually better when you came. I only came from oral sex and some clients were quite good at it. I wasn't sure why I couldn't come during sex, but it didn't really bother me — I still enjoyed the sensation.

Pleasure moved through my body in waves as I came in his mouth. He seemed pleased that I'd enjoyed it, and he got on top of me and started thrusting away. He came in a matter of minutes; his erection hadn't been that strong but it didn't seem to matter. He lay very still on top of me and I wondered whether he'd had a heart attack. I'd heard stories from Queensland about old clients dying in bookings from the excitement, but luckily my client was only resting while he got his breath back.

As soon as I saw him out and tidied my room, it was on to the next introduction and the next client. It was a Monday night and there were only three girls working, including myself. Since I was new everyone wanted to see me, except for the other girls' regulars, who were staying faithful. I'd heard that some of the girls didn't use condoms with some regulars, so they kept on going back to them. I never knew whether to believe it or not.

When I went back to the introduction-room there was a cute blonde guy and a friend waiting with him. He wanted to see me and I couldn't believe anyone so cute wanted to pay for sex, and wanted to pay me for it as well. It seemed ironic that in England I couldn't get any sex and now I

had men paying for it. I'd been such a mixed-up kid, insecure about my looks, with a really low self-esteem — I
thought that no-one would ever want me. My mum and
brother would always tease me about becoming an old spin-
ster, looking after mum in my old age and I believed them.
Now I knew that wasn't true — I had lots of catching-up
to do.

I gladly took him through to one of the rooms where
he gave me the money. At reception, Suzie lifted her eye-
brows as if to say 'You'll enjoy this one'. I rushed back to
the room where he was waiting with a towel around his
waist. I didn't know what to say or do. He came over to me
and we started kissing. He unzipped my dress from behind and I reached down to feel his crotch underneath
the towel. I felt really shy and confessed that I hadn't been
working for long. He told me not to worry because he was
going to be really gentle. My dress slipped to the ground,
as did his towel, and he sat down on the bed next to me
and bent down to kiss my nipples. He sucked and licked
until I had to pull him away because he was sending me
into a frenzy of passion. I reached again for his cock and
got down on my knees to take it into my mouth. I wanted
him inside me so badly I was aching. But he wouldn't let
me have him until he'd fingered and licked my pussy, and
I was lying down on the bed somewhere close to heaven
when he slipped his cock inside and thrust into me, back
and forth, back and forth. I reached behind to grab his
buttocks so I could pull him further into me. We carried
on long past the booking time and Suzie had to buzz me
several times before we stopped.

If all the bookings were like that I would probably have

worked forever. Unfortunately they weren't; in fact a lot of them were quite damaging. Some of the bookings I would rather have forgotten, but just like any other bad memory they are always lurking there, somewhere in my mind.

A booking could easily turn into rape if the client was aggressive or drunk or just hard to control. Because I was so new to working, I was never sure how far to let the client go. At A Dab of Perfume there were times when I would rather have left the room and not be paid than put up with the client taking his shit out on me.

I remember one booking I was conned into. It was the same night I'd seen the cute guy. Towards the end of the night there was a crowd of drunks waiting for an introduction from the girls. I'd told Suzie that I didn't want to see anyone who was drunk, but she insisted that these clients had just been at a business dinner, and had only had a few drinks. I believed her and took one of them through into the rooms, even though it looked as if he'd drunk far too much. He kept on asking stupid questions and trying to feel my body before he'd paid. I was annoyed at his behaviour, and told him that I didn't want any trouble. He just started laughing and tried to grab my breasts again. He said he wanted to see my tits so he knew what he was paying for.

I took his money and decided that I'd get the booking over and done with as soon as possible. It was money after all. Back in the room he was just stumbling out of the shower when I walked in. He staggered over to me, mumbling that now he could have me, and started pulling my dress down. He put his hands on my breasts and pulled at my nipples and commented on my small tits. He went to suck them and his teeth bit into the nipples and sent a sharp pain down through my body.

I pushed his mouth off me and tried to squirm away from him. The more I tried to get his hands and mouth off me, the more he persisted. I regretted doing the booking and I tried to switch off so it wouldn't feel so bad. Every move he made on my body hurt and every smart comment rang in my ears and hurt as well. I didn't really know how to distance myself from the bad clients. How could you? You were in the room with them.

I got down to the business of getting him off. His erection kept on going up and down because he'd drunk too much, and the more I tried to make it hard by sucking on it or trying to push it into my vagina, the more it went down. This seemed to go on for hours, and he pulled and grabbed at my body as if it was a piece of meat. I felt cheated and badly done by, but what was I to do? I was after all a hooker, and this type of thing came with the job.

At the end of the night I'd made four hundred dollars. I saw a few more clients after the drunk, and most of them had been middle-aged men. They'd all been nice, after that one disaster, and I didn't feel quite so upset when I left to go back to my hotel room.

I slept through into the day and got up to go for a walk and get something to eat. By the time I had finished wandering around it was night and I had to get ready to go back to work again. I'd catch a taxi there and the taxi drivers would all know that I was a hooker as soon as I mentioned the address. I didn't really care whether they knew or not, but I hated the questions — how long have you worked for, etc, etc. I wasn't smart enough to tell them that I was just the receptionist or something other than a prostitute. The taxi drivers seemed all for prostitutes, and their attitudes were usually good, if a little sleazy, but I squirm at the thought of how many I actually told what I was doing, when the questions started. Although I knew that it was not a good idea to advertise that you were a prostitute, I never really kept it to myself.

There were more girls working this time, and we each took our turn getting the clients, unless they especially wanted someone else; that way everyone got to make some money. I never really bonded with the other working girls: I was very shy and quiet and only really joined in the conversation occasionally. They would usually talk about their boyfriends and work and themselves. I told them about George, the reason I'd come to Canberra. They all thought I was wasting my time.

Every time a working girl gave me advice she was right. I don't know whether it was working in such a tough industry that had made them so worldly. I'd always been a disappointed dreamer, but they obviously had had their fair share of reality, to know that life wasn't exactly a bed of roses.

When I was having sex with the clients in the room, I always used to think about how much money I was making. It was like having a giant calculator in my head. If the client was doing something I didn't like, I'd pretend that I really liked it, or else it would become too much to bear. Unless I liked them, I hated clients sucking my breasts and it became my pet hate. I would rather them lick my pussy for hours than suck on my nipples. Every girl was different. Some girls didn't mind sucking the guys off, and letting them come in their mouths, but at the same time they wouldn't let them go down on them. I kept my service pretty straight. I didn't mind kissing, although I knew it was a pretty good way to catch a cold, but I never actually caught anything drastic from it.

Since Canberra was full of politicians, I'd been expecting a few requests for bondage. I'd never really got that close to whips before, but I'd read many times in England — and seen the pictures — of famous politicians caught in the act of being tied up and humiliated by a hooker.

The closest I came to this was when I got a booking with a client who'd brought along his own pain device, an elastic band. He was a strange looking guy, with his eyes bulging out of his face, and once we were naked on the bed he encouraged me to pull the elastic band tighter over his balls. He then got on the floor and wanted me to stamp on his cock. I was afraid I'd burst one of his blood vessels but his cock withstood my weight and he loved every second of it. The more pain I applied the harder his cock became. I was amazed that anyone could get off on so much pain. I had had no experience of it and the saying that 'there's a fine line between pleasure and pain' didn't mean a thing to me back then. I just thought he was weird. He told me he'd been a full-time slave to a mistress before, and she used to torture him in her dungeon all the time. It seemed quite bizarre to me — I'd always been pretty straight.

After I'd twisted his cock around a bit more he came, and all his come — and there was so much of it — squirted out all over the bed. He complimented me on my excellent bondage skills and asked me whether I was interested in his becoming my full-time slave. Needless to say I declined his offer.

I still had my mind on George all the time — I thought in some way he'd make all the difference. I imagined that as soon as he found out I was in Canberra, he'd take me back into his arms and somehow we'd live happily ever after.

I couldn't have been more wrong as I discovered when I went looking for him in a nightclub that everyone went to on a Saturday night. A taxi driver who had picked me up outside another club, which had about six people in it, told me about it. If George was going to be anywhere he'd be there. For hours I stood drinking or wandering around watching the people dance. Then I saw him. He was going up the stairs — my gorgeous George.

I tapped him on the shoulder and as he turned around I smiled. He didn't even smile back or acknowledge me in any way at all; he just kept on walking up the stairs. I was about to go after him when one of his friends, whom I recognised from Queensland, pulled me aside and told me that George was here with his girlfriend. I told him I'd come to Canberra specially to find George. I must have sounded like a fruitcake when I was rambling on about how much I loved him, even though I'd only known him for about a week — I was pretty drunk. We went straight to the bar and I gulped down four drinks straight and started pouring my heart out again. George's friend quite liked me and by the end of the night I was kissing him out of sheer loneliness. But the only one I wanted was George.

I didn't really want to stay in Canberra after that, even

though it was a nice relaxing place — I felt I had to move on. I told them at A Dab of Perfume that I was leaving, and they said they were sorry to hear I was going, and I'd be welcome back any time, especially during the holiday season when it got really busy.

It had been an experience working there, but it wasn't a great place to make money. The girls were all paid weekly, and even though I'd earned over a thousand dollars that week, almost half of it was taken out for tax by Suzie's husband, who doubled up as the accountant. I was amazed that the girls kept on working there when I was sure there would be places where the tax would be lower and you would actually have something to show for all those nights when your pussy was left sore and your spirits left low.

Chapter 3

Flowers for sale

Once again I was on the move, and this time I decided to go to Sydney. I booked ahead to stay at an inner-city hotel but I couldn't have anticipated how grotty it would be. I could easily have stayed at an expensive hotel, as most working girls would, but I never saw the money I made from sleeping with men as easy.

The girls in Canberra had recommended Lilies as an excellent brothel to work at. It was apparently one of the busiest places in Sydney, but the girls all had horror stories about it. I even had vague memories of hearing the name in Queensland. So I went to have a look, to see what all the fuss was about. Some of the girls had said that Lilies was really strict, there were rules for this and that, and you weren't even allowed to talk to the other girls. But they stayed because the money was so good.

I caught a taxi there and it stopped outside a large Victorian house in Surry Hills. There were bars on the windows and the curtains were drawn. I pressed the door bell and waited outside the huge red door. A heavily made-up receptionist answered, and took me through to one of the waiting rooms. Walking down the corridor I couldn't help but notice how everything was decorated in red — even the lighting was red.

The receptionist came back with a form and some questions. The first was how long had I worked? Then, did I do fantasies? Would I do bi-twins (two girls together)? Was I gay or straight? Did I have a boyfriend? A girlfriend? The questions went on and I became irritated by it all. Normally to get a job in a brothel, you just needed a cunt and a mouth and that was it — you had the job.

She told me that there were twenty girls on each shift and we all had to wear strictly after-eight clothing, and have full make-up, stockings and stilettos. What I found the most exasperating was that it was compulsory to let the clients go down on you (without any protection) and if you didn't agree to do it, you couldn't start. Where was the safety from diseases in that?

I went back to my hotel room to take a bath, and get something to eat. Then I set about getting half-ready to go to work. It would be better than staying at this dismal, depressing hotel and what else was I going to do? I didn't know anyone in Sydney.

Lilies was turning out to be everything that I'd heard

about and more. I remembered the girl in Queensland who'd gone to work at a similar place and she'd lasted a day. She had said all the receptionists were bitches who treated you like shit, and they had too many rules. And so it seemed. The night I started I brought along two dresses and the hostess at the time said neither was good enough — I'd have to hire one of the house dresses for twenty dollars, which would come out of the money that I earned that night. The dress I took was a brightly coloured glamorous number.

When I went back to get changed, I looked around at the other working girls, in various stages of undress and make-up application. Their ages varied from teenagers to late thirties. Some were beautiful but most were just pretty or even ordinary. But after we all got ready and sat in the adjoining waiting-room, ready for inspection, everyone looked really great. Masses of very feminine clothes, make-up, hair, accessories, wigs, high heels, perfume — anything that could make a woman look beautiful, was there. It was almost like cheating: we'd transformed ourselves from normal looking everyday women into vampy whores of the night.

The hostesses looked around at us all and checked our make-up and hair, and made sure everything was in place. One of them said that Peter, the owner of Lilies, was ready to see his girls, so she led us through to the girls' waiting-room, where we'd spend our time until six in the morning when we weren't in bookings. There were twenty of us, all squeezed together, practically elbowing each other for space, with only a small television to watch. There was an adjoining kitchen that had a supply of cola and rabbit-type diet food, which we paid twenty dollars a night for.

I'd been told beforehand that conversation between the girls must be kept to chit-chat, since our involvement had to be with clients, not with each other. So as the girls chit-chatted about the price of dresses, or their favourite hair-piece of the moment, the owner, Peter, and one of his low-life sidekicks made their grand entrance. It was quite obvious they'd been doing more than enough lines of cocaine, and yet the owner looked like one of those proper, rich Greek doctors. From their sleazy stares and dull jokes, I summed them up as jerk-off pimps with nothing better to do than make money out of girls.

They rocked back and forth on the balls of their feet, like bouncers do at nightclubs, and made comments about how we were a lazy bunch of thieving bitches, that we were always turning up late for work and slacking off. Peter's tone went up and down as he really started getting into the conversation (it must have been killer cocaine), and his side-kick chimed in that if he caught any of us thieving from the girls' room he'd smash our faces in.

As they departed, with a cheery 'Have a good night ladies', everyone sighed as if God had just left the room. It seemed incredible that a boss, even though he was a pimp, could talk to us like that; I was amazed that the girls put up with it. So it seemed that the horror stories about Lilies were true.

But the place was beautiful. Everywhere was lavishly decorated from all the girls' hard-earned money that they fucked for. There were sixteen rooms altogether, upstairs and downstairs. Some were double rooms with spas and bars, with beautiful marble floors and leather beds, and television sets and videos for watching pornos. It was here the client could be pampered. Then there were the orgy rooms for two couples or more, filled with gigantic beds with pillows scattered all over them. It was quite intimidating to have to look beautiful enough to compliment the surroundings.

Upstairs was more basic; there were four rooms with just beds, a shower, television and video, but nicely decorated. They were for the clients who couldn't afford to be spoilt; there was no bar, no spa, just plain old boring sex.

At first, when we went to do our introductions, I was nervous, standing in front of a man, or a group of men, wondering who'd be picked. Each girl would introduce herself and then we'd wait in line while the client made his choice. I did about four introductions before I was chosen; I was feeling a bit intimidated so I'd say my name really quietly, without smiling. This annoyed the receptionist, as she knew that with young looks and a good body I could easily make a lot of money. She pulled me through into the girls' changing-room and sat me down and started to rub foundation all over my face. I told her to leave my face alone; I was quite capable of putting on my own make-up. But she was furious and said that I hadn't applied enough.

I brushed her aside and this time I made a huge effort with the introductions so the bitchy hostesses would leave me alone, but it paid off, as I started getting lots of bookings. Since I was only twenty, I still had the freshness and innocence of someone young, and I suppose that's what the clients wanted.

I was still very nervous during the bookings, and that's

what kept me good in the room. I wasn't complacent or bored, because I found that, while the sex was very routine, some of it was still quite exciting. The most exciting part of all was being chosen from twenty other girls. It was like a compliment, a great ego booster. Most of the girls looked very beautiful with their make-up and clothes, and to realise that you stood out among them was flattering, even if the guy was a jerk.

In England, I had very low self-esteem; I truly believed I was very ugly — my brother had always said I was. Once when I was going through a bad stage during puberty, he managed to convince me that my face was that ugly I locked myself in my room for days, miserable, sure that he was right. But since I'd started working, guys had kept saying, 'Oh, you're beautiful, you should be a model'. And even if it was bullshit, it made me feel more confident about my image. Most clients really appreciated my body and even made flattering comments about my vagina, which I'd always thought was pretty average.

I still had problems getting undressed even though I'd now worked on the Gold Coast and in Canberra. The clients found it quite charming and not at all like a working girl, especially in a place like Lilies that was very much a well-known brothel.

It was fun to go in the spa for some bookings, even though there was an incredible amount of chlorine in there. It was great to just lie back and relax with a drink. If the client was okay it could be very enjoyable. I also got more money for those bookings. For a minimum stay of three quarters of an hour I'd get one hundred dollars and the other hundred would go to Lilies. For an hour I'd get one hundred and fifty, while for seeing a client in the smaller rooms I'd only get fifty for half an hour and one hundred for an hour. So when we got a client we would take them straight into the spa room and try and get them to stay there.

I was lucky; I was getting lots of clients who liked the spa rooms and most of them kept coming back to see me. I was so busy I'd go in at eight at night and I'd have clients waiting for me all the time. It was like being top cat. I had put a huge effort into the bookings and it was paying off. Each night I was working, I was clearing five hundred dollars, and because it was illegal in Sydney, there was no tax to pay. I would go home and count the piles of money on the bed. Back then it was like having a million dollars and I thought I was quite mature, earning so much. Now I knew why girls put up with Lilies; it was the addiction to money.

There were listening devices in all the rooms to make sure we weren't over-charging the client and agreeing to do anal sex, which was strictly forbidden. And tips were supposed to be handed in at Lilies and split because that was also part of the deal, but I just stuffed them in my knickers. I'd always talk loudly with the clients about the staff, hoping that they'd listen in to what I was saying. I knew the receptionists disliked me but I didn't really care.

Generally, I was quite easy-going in the bookings. I'd never give head without a condom but I'd let the guys kiss me because it was something most of the other working girls wouldn't do, and I didn't mind. I'd let them lick my pussy if they seemed nice — that was still my favourite part of the booking — and if they were good at it. I always gave in to pleasure when this happened; I'd just lie back, relax and enjoy it.

Few of my clients were good-looking, but sex just became sex when someone was paying for it. There was always that feeling that you had to perform, and make sure they were having a good time, and this made it hard to relax.

Since I was quite anti-drugs, and wouldn't take them during my working time, I found it really hard to stay awake at night, still having sex and being entertaining. I hardly felt a thing with any of the men, and even though someone might be sticking a huge cock inside me, it never really felt that great after a while. The best part about working at Lilies was that sense of being the messed-up working girl, but making lots of money from it, thank you very much. You could agonise about why you were doing it, but the real reason had an awful lot to do with money.

I decided to leave the hole I was living in, and I wondered where I would go next. I had learned a lot about money and clients and survival of the fittest, and things that I would never have encountered before. At times I'd felt like a glamorous movie star, and at other times like a whore. After a while I felt at a low ebb from the long nights and too many clients at Lilies. It was time to leave, and I recalled that a girl had mentioned a place in Melbourne that was good to work at.

Chapter 4

Working Melbourne

Coming into Melbourne was like taking a breath of fresh air. I'd been avoiding visiting Melbourne because on the soaps, back in England, the weather had always looked cold and rainy, and I'd really come to Australia for warm weather. But once the train came into the city I felt I was more at home than ever. The sky loomed in all it's nightly beauty and I had that feeling of anticipation again. The air was fresh and crisp, a nice change from the humidity of Sydney and Queensland.

By the beach in St. Kilda I booked into a serviced apartment I'd found listed in the Yellow Pages. After I dumped my suitcases on the floor, I went down to the bottle shop next door to grab a bottle of ouzo. I knew there were plenty of nightclubs in Melbourne and it was considered by some more of a party town than Sydney. I got ready and caught a cab down to a club listed in the tourist guide. It was Friday night after all.

I'd been standing at the bar by myself for half an hour when a young Greek guy joined me. We talked and sat down on the couches to drink bourbon and coke. I thought about taking him back to my hotel room and fucking him. He looked okay and as we kissed and he fondled my breasts, my pussy became dripping wet. When he bent down to kiss my breasts I coyly tried to hide him under my jacket as he sucked on my nipples. I felt his cock underneath his trousers and he was bulging hard. The music pounding from the dance floor added to the excitement, and no-one seemed to notice as he undid the buttons on my jeans and poked his fingers inside my cunt. Thrusting in and out he carried on sucking my tits — I felt so turned on.

He was a carpenter by trade, he told me, as he gave me a lift back to my apartment in his working van. I just wanted his cock inside me and I didn't care about anything else. I'd drunk too much and was feeling really horny.

Once we got inside my place everything went downhill. He took his clothes off and revealed his incredible bulging muscles but he had a rash all over his body. When he fucked me it was like having sandpaper rubbed all over my chest, but then we did it in doggy style and it was all over in a matter of minutes. I was left feeling unsatisfied, but he slept next to me for the rest of the night and it felt nice having someone there. I was glad I had come to Melbourne.

I needed somewhere to work so, in the morning when

my one night stand had left, I searched the ads in a paper where the brothels advertised. There were hundreds of brothels in Melbourne and escort agencies and I was at a loss as to which one to work for. I chose one in the city that sounded okay and called up to see whether they needed any new girls. Brothels always wanted new girls: they brought in the clients.

This brothel was an old terrace house that was cold and musty inside. A young receptionist showed me around and told me the prices and rules. Drugs were strictly forbidden and we had a bag search before and after we started work. There were four different shifts I could work since the place was open twenty-four hours. The rooms were neat and tidy but were cheaply decorated. Towels were stacked inside each room ready for all the clients. If I wanted, she said, I could start that night. I decided on the six to midnight shift to begin with — I was sick of late nights.

The owner was a Greek guy, who popped in the night I started. He offered me the good advice of saving money, and keeping away from drugs. He said he'd seen a lot of girls messed up on drugs in Melbourne, and they always ended up wasting money on the needle or on their using boyfriends.

The clients came in early and I got my first twenty-minute booking straight away. He'd just finished work and he only wanted a quickie. He was quite young and good-looking and when he took his clothes off he had a nice firm body and smooth skin. I moaned with pleasure as his cock slid inside me for fifteen minutes, and then he came with some frantic thrusting after the receptionist had buzzed to say his time was up. The sex was always good at the beginning of the shift and if there was some sort of attraction, it was the same as having unpaid sex.

But once again the money wasn't that good. The house took half of what we made which wasn't exactly much. I did a succession of quickies, and a one hour, which added up to about one hundred and twenty dollars after tax. There wasn't much to show for all that effort, but at least I got to go home early.

I slept alone in my bed and went into the city the next morning, mooching around the shopping centre and department stores. I could always find something that I wanted to buy and I loved spending money on clothes and make-up, things I could never afford before. I was still only twenty and even a hundred dollars seemed quite a lot — that's why I didn't mind fucking three men to get it.

It was cold in Melbourne, and the second night I worked the wind blew through the laundry into the girls' tiny lounge-room while we waited for introductions. We'd huddle together on the fraying old couches and watch as girls would come out of their booking. Everytime they'd go through into the laundry an icy chill would dance through our skimpy clothes. The microwave would be buzzing away in the corner next to the coffees and teas, warming up some greasy sandwich from the local take-away.

It was kind of depressing sitting around doing nothing, waiting, even though there was a television to watch. The other girls were a mixture of personalities. Some had worked for a while, and they seemed quite settled; nothing really stirred them. But some of them looked so tired and old and it seemed they'd worked too long. A few were drug users and only got away with working there because they were so popular and got the clients to stay. They would doze off in the lounge-room and were prone to throwing up in the room if they'd had bad smack. Some of them looked so pale and sick, and after a hit it was hard for them to make any sense.

For a prostitute I was still quite tame. I wore minimum make-up and moderate dresses for work. I looked innocent, naive and young. The clients usually went for it, but there were other girls working there who looked better than I did. As I was learning, if a girl was stunning or stood out amongst the rest, you might as well kiss your shift goodbye. It wasn't fair that the money that you earned depended so much on how you looked. I could feel very insecure by the end of the night if I hadn't been chosen often. In Sydney, I'd been used to earning lots of money and getting most of the clients, but now the price had been dropped and I wasn't getting as many. One or two of the girls had more visually grabbing features. One had beautiful, real blonde waist-length hair and a petite figure, and others must have just looked more appealing to the clients that came here.

I thought about changing brothels. I'd made my mind up to stay in Melbourne but I didn't want to stay here. I remembered the girls at Lilies who had told me about the Golden Gate, which was supposed to be another high-class brothel. Anything was better than sitting in a draughty old terrace house fucking men for thirty dollars. You could die in a place like that.

As it turned out, the Golden Gate was a better alternative and it had the reputation of being a cool place to work. The taxi driver who drove me there said the most beautiful girls in Melbourne worked at the Golden Gate; it was like the cream of prostitutes, and indeed I noticed it was very grand as the taxi driver pulled up outside. In fact I felt quite intimidated by its hugeness and the aura of it all.

Walking inside to the reception area I looked at the marble floors and black leather couches that decorated the entrance. Everything looked so elegant, including the receptionists with white painted faces who dressed in black suits. They smiled up from their desk, and asked me to take a seat while they buzzed through for a hostess to come and show me around.

A tiny, beautiful woman with Rhonda written on a name badge appeared from the entrance and smiled warmly at me. She was death-white with jet-black hair pulled back in a bun. She beckoned me to come through and have the grand tour of the building, which looked more like a flash nightclub than a brothel.

The lounge-room was huge; tables and chairs were scattered everywhere and there were pool tables, and a juke-box that stood belting out hits, and even a swimming pool in the adjoining room. Even though it had sophisticated surroundings, the atmosphere was relaxing and the girls sat around the lounge chatting casually to each other. There weren't many clients as it was still early afternoon, but, as Rhonda explained, it got very busy at night and they had up to twenty girls working on the weekend.

The rooms were all beautiful and no expense had been spared in their decoration. It was like a huge mansion that had been transformed into a sex retreat for men with hard-ons and plenty of money. There were spa rooms, ordinary rooms, executive rooms, orgy rooms — just about every room you could think of. As Rhonda explained the different prices, she told me how much money I would get for the different bookings.

She stopped outside the girls' changing-room and turned quite suddenly towards me and said, with a very serious look on her face, 'Working here is like being a model. You have to look glamorous and gorgeous to get the clients, hair and make-up have to be perfect, and the clothes you wear have to be eyecatching'. There was no-one who looked like a model in the changing-room as we went inside and looked around; they must have all been fucking in the rooms, I mused. She led me back to the reception area, looked down the roster and said I could start that night. She said we had to work a minimum of four shifts a week, one of which had to be in the day and the other a weekend night. There were other rules too: we were checked to see whether we shaved our legs and underarms each shift we worked, and it was compulsory to paint our fingernails and toenails. Was it meant to be a sign of elegance or did just too many working girls have ugly ingrown toenails?

I thought I'd make as much money at the Golden Gate as I had at Lilies. It seemed more relaxing and, even though they had rules, the receptionists didn't bark at you as they did at Lilies. The only difference at the Golden Gate was that you had to actually socialise with clients to get the booking and that meant chatting them up. I wasn't used to chatting up men; I was more used to having them chat me up, so when I started that night I was in for a nasty shock when men didn't exactly flock to my side. The girls who were working all looked beautiful and elegant, but it was so dark it wouldn't have really mattered even if they weren't. What mattered here was an outgoing personality —wall-flowers weren't noticed.

I got my first booking with a house regular who wanted to stay for half an hour. I was wearing the reject dress they didn't like at Lilies and it must have been bringing me good luck, because I hadn't been talking much to men in the lounge-room. House regulars were always easy to see; they knew the score, and most just went through the routine of brothel sex, which is always very predictable. First there was the back massage, the tongue massage, which is optional (depending on the girl). Then the client rolls over and usually at this stage the cock's hard, the condom's ready to put on and it's into the girl's mouth, then into her pussy. Then the client comes and relaxes while the girl adds up how much money she's made so far that night.

Although the Golden Gate was expensively decorated, the prices were not outrageously high. For half an hour it was one hundred and twenty and then for an hour it was one hundred and ninety. This attracted a variety of clients, most of whom were businessmen, but then you had the nine-to-fivers, students, drunks, tradespeople, some guys on the dole who had saved up to come in, dealers, sportspeople, famous people, just about anyone and everyone came to have a look and book the girls.

Some girls would get really paranoid that someone they knew would come in and recognise them as they walked around entertaining and trying to pick up clients. They went to great lengths to disguise themselves in wigs and heavy make-up, and at the end of the night they looked quite different in their natural state. I, on the other hand, was lucky that I was new to Melbourne and didn't have to worry about anyone recognising me yet.

As I was to find, once a week the girls had a pep talk with the manager, Richard, who was in charge of all the girls. He was cute and gay and he sat in his nice big office and checked the girls for needlemarks (no junkies allowed) and weighed them, to see that they weren't putting on weight. There would also be a discussion about how many regulars you had, and if you didn't get regulars you were out. They wanted girls who brought the clients in and made them the most money. And if you couldn't do that then there would always be someone ready to take your place.

After a week I hadn't really done so well, inspite of a good start, being the new girl. The easy bookings died off and I was struggling to get two or three a night. There were so many other girls and they were all good at chatting men up. I found it difficult relating to the clients when all I really wanted was their money. The night always dragged on and it was hard to keep awake so late. Some girls took speed to keep awake and others just did it on coffee, and some probably took just about anything they could lay their hands on, but I never really got into that.

I did have some new experiences working at the Golden Gate; I had my first orgy booking there. The room was huge with three double beds, a spa and double showers. The other two girls had worked for a long time and were old hands at group bookings, whereas I hadn't done it before. The three men who chose us were all quite drunk; they were business men and in their late thirties. After the money was taken care of (and there seemed so much of it) the guys showered and we all jumped into the spa together. I felt embarassed being naked in front of the other girls and hid my body under the water.

The other girls' bodies were well-rounded and they seemed confident and at ease in the booking. My client was very eager and cornered me in the spa with a hard on. But he couldn't keep it up once we got into the bed, and I was dismayed when the other girls had practically got their clients off and I couldn't even start.

Then he started. He told me it was my fault he couldn't get it off. He wanted a real woman, he said, and he reached over to touch the other voluptuous girl lying beside her client. They had only paid for one girl each so they weren't allowed to touch or swap girls. I felt so degraded; I was naked and vulnerable and here I had some drunk telling me I wasn't good enough to get him off. As I put another condom on his weak erection I buried my face between his thighs and cried. He kept on saying it was my fault as he reached over to touch the other girl and she kept telling him to lay off or pay extra money. No one seemed to notice my tears as they rolled down my cheeks and I felt like drowning myself in the spa.

At the end of the booking I was still left on the bed with him while everyone else had taken showers and were in the middle of getting dressed. His friends kept joking around and throwing encouraging remarks while we remained silent except for my sniffles coming from between his legs. At the end of it all, he decided to book the other girl, who was able to turn him on more than I could. I showered, got dressed and went back to the girls' room where I burst out crying.

Rhonda was there and she asked me what was wrong. Everything was wrong, I wanted to tell her, but I just muttered something about a drunk client and asked whether I could go home early. What I wanted to say was that I couldn't handle this job. Just seeing other girls fucking in the room and doing what I'd been doing for the last few months really brought home to me what a fucked job it really was. I couldn't handle having to do what it took to be a hooker. There were so many bad clients, but instead of giving up right then, I just went home, cried, spent the next day comforting myself by doing nothing, and then went back to work. But I decided not to do group bookings again.

Chapter 5

Do you believe in fate?

It was while I was working at Decadence, a brothel that I'd found out about from the girls at the Golden Gate, that I met my future husband. Decadence was much smaller and cosier, and there was no need to chat the clients up beforehand; it was strictly introduction only. That made a big difference. I'd slipped down to a few bookings the last few weeks at the Golden Gate, and I'd left without even saying goodbye. It didn't really matter anyway; there was always another young face ready to take your place.

Getting bookings at Decadence was a lot easier; the girls weren't nearly as glamorous as at the Golden Gate and they didn't take themselves so seriously. There were two South American girls in their thirties, a few Asian girls, Australians and an Italian. Natasha, a twentyish Australian was the most attractive of us all. I learnt from the other girls that if she was on a shift she would get all the introductions. I could see why — she was blond and busty and had an otherwise petite body that all of the clients seemed to like.

The shifts went until three in the morning and at the weekends until five. We were to wear nothing but lingerie and stockings and suspenders, and of course high heels to complete the look. On the first night that I started working, the manageress took me aside and into her office. She asked me whether I needed any training with my sexual technique, because she had ladies who specialised in coaching the girls to perform in the room. I thought I knew pretty much what I needed to know about sex. After all, practice makes perfect and having sex was all that I had been doing.

On my nights off I still kept going out to clubs searching for a potential de facto. I'd been in Australia now for eight months and my visa would soon expire. On one particular night when I'd been drinking lots, I was leaning down from a balcony, transfixed by the sea of bodies dancing below, when a young Greek boy standing next to me said something like — you look out of it. I answered back, yes I am, which seemed a suitable answer to a rude comment. He introduced himself as Mark and when I looked around I smiled because I realised he was with a guy I'd met in one of the clubs in Canberra when I had been looking for George.

In an instant, they started arguing over me without any thought about whom I might want. I wasn't interested in the guy from Canberra — he hadn't been able to do much for me then — so when Mark asked me to dance, we went downstairs and left his friend sulking by himself. Mark was an enthusiastic dancer and I watched him move his arms in weird circular movements and kick his legs out. Afterwards we moved upstairs to the couches where we started kissing. Even though I'd been having lots of sex recently I still loved the simple sensation of kissing, of hands reaching for my breasts underneath my clothes, and of feeling a hard cock underneath trousers. We stayed there for hours, getting off on each others' bodies, then drank some more and stayed longer, talking to each other. He liked my accent and he loved the fact that I was from England. He told me that he'd grown up in Australia, of Cypriot parents, and that he was at university full-time, studying engineering. He said he was twenty-five but I was to learn later from his licence that he was really only twenty-one. He knew his friend — the one I'd met before in Canberra — from being in the Army Reserves together, and they'd been best friends for years.

From what I was learning about Mark, he was very easy-going and down to earth. Or so it seemed. He was from a nice Greek background, he was good-looking and a good kisser, and I was terribly impressed that he was going to university — I had a fetish for intelligent men. I lied, and told him I was a secretary and that I was on a working holiday in Australia for one year, and that I'd be going home in December.

He gave me his number and I said I'd call him. Just as I was stepping into a taxi I dropped the piece of paper with his number on it, and just by the merest chance found it on the pavement before we drove away. It must have been fate.

As it turned out the two South American girls I was working with were living next to me in the Toorak apartments, as were a few other working girls (it was easy to get a lease there). One of them could hardly speak any English, so it was fun trying to teach her. She was probably the friendliest working girl I had met. She was hilarious to talk to because she had to mime and mimic everything to explain herself. I knew that she was supporting a family she had back home. Each girl had a de facto they'd paid money to, to get residency and stay in the country, and they'd met both of them while working in brothels. It seemed like a good idea, and it would solve the problem of lying behind someone's back about what I was doing for a living. So I started to work more shifts in a week in hope of finding someone to help me.

I was earning okay money and we were lucky at Decadence because we didn't have any tax to pay, just fifty dollars a week for credit card clearance. I got into a routine of sleeping more in the day so I could work better at night. Most girls looked tired when they came in to work. I don't think many of them took heavy drugs but quite a few looked as if they could have been heavy dope-smokers.

Do you believe in fate?

Although I hadn't initially wanted to, I started doing quite a few double bookings. I still felt embarrassed and uncomfortable about being naked before another girl and having to perform. And I still had the bad memory from the Golden Gate and the orgy booking I'd done there.

I did a booking with two Japanese guys just back from being on the town. One couldn't speak any English, and the other one was his tourist guide. I knew between them they were bound to cause problems. They wanted a double with myself and another girl, Ginger. It had been a quiet night so I decided to go ahead and do it, regardless of how uncomfortable I knew I would feel.

In the booking I managed to relax, and once we got on the bed we started massaging and rubbing our breasts all over them. I had the tour guide and she had the drunk. Even though I was not particularly interested in female bodies, Ginger seemed quite eager to share her body with me. She brushed her breasts up against me and it was nice to feel soft flesh. We giggled and acted like school-kids and the Japanese guys loved it. The booking was probably the most professional I had ever done, with all the oohs and aahs in the right places; normally I never bothered. On nights when I was tired, guys would fuck me and I would be totally silent.

We turned the clients over and put condoms on their cocks. I watched Ginger tickle her tongue along her client's balls. I hated licking their balls but some girls didn't mind. I sucked on my client's cock but it wouldn't go hard enough. I watched as Ginger sat on her client's cock and fucked him. She leaned back and ground her thighs into him. He made the appropriate grunting sounds until he came. I was still working on my guy's hard-on when Ginger pulled her guy's cock out and there was no condom on it. She started shouting at him, 'Where's the condom? Where's the condom?' He just laughed back at her while she frantically started looking for it. When she found the condom empty next to him on the bed she waved it in his face, and he responded in broken English that there was more feeling without the condom.

He'd come inside her and put her at risk of catching something as well as getting pregnant. I couldn't believe he could be that stupid, even if he was drunk. I felt sorry for her, but the client just carried on laughing as she jumped into the shower and frantically squirted water inside herself. We pulled out of the booking and Ginger went home distressed. It was just another case of lousy job, high risk and no gratitude.

There were good and bad clients all the time. Most of them were fine at Decadence and it was never busy enough to make my body that tired. I liked bookings where the guys were gentle and soft and especially when they liked to lick my pussy. I hated clients who were too drunk because they always caused problems. Some clients were weird, some had mental diseases, but a lot were just lonely and some were actually looking for love. But most just wanted to fuck someone without any hassles.

On my nights off I kept seeing Mark. He turned out to be a really nice guy and the more I saw him the more I liked him. He kept on telling me he wasn't going to be one of those guys who would sponsor a woman into the country, which was quite funny really because I'd never asked him, and had no intention of doing so at the time. I knew he liked me a lot. He said I was different from all of his other girlfriends and I think the fact that I gave great head probably had something to do with it too.We used to have sex in his car after going out and I was always so horny and ready to fuck, even though I was working four nights at a brothel. Sex was always exciting in the beginning and the fact that I was attracted to Mark made a big difference. We would fuck for hours in his car until he couldn't have sex any more.

I showed him how to lick my pussy properly, and I'd kiss and tease his cock for hours. He was kind and considerate and he always held me and made me feel normal again. He and his friends, who were all from university, put me into the real world and made me forget about prostitution and home and what I was going to do.

I hadn't come from a settled family. My mum had brought my brother and me up alone in a house in the country. My father had committed suicide when I was three or four. I never knew why he killed himself but my grandmother, on my mother's side, had told me he was crazy, and was in and out of mental hospitals, as was his mother. Gran had showed me a clipping from the newspaper about how he had drowned himself in the river. My mum had never mentioned anything about him except that he was evil, and that was all she would say. There was one picture of him at home, and he looked exactly like my brother when he was older.

My mum had violent boyfriend after violent boyfriend when I was young, and I always remembered her crawling into bed with me, terrified, with blood all over her. I hated watching her get beaten up and I always had a feeling of hopelessness. I often retreated into my own world of fantasy and I remember thinking how the world was a beautiful, mystical place and I couldn't wait to grow up. Unfortunately, I was only five and I had a long time to go.

I became the object of my brother's anger: he was an unhappy child from the day he was born. I knew that quite a few times he'd got in the way of my mother's boyfriends, and had been beaten up quite badly. As soon as I started school, and he was about nine and I was five, he began letting his friends touch me. I remember a lot of it very vividly. I would always be tricked into an empty barn or field, or behind a car, and they would pull my pants down and start sticking their fingers into my vagina. My brother would become fascinated with my fanny, as he called it back then, and would try and stick his fingers in the furthest.

Everywhere I turned there would always be boys wanting to play with me. One of them was a neighbour about ten years older than my brother and the rest were my brother's best friends. The abuse went on until I was about nine and old enough to say no. I forgot about it after that, but I think it was always in my heart.

Mark and I went away together for a weekend on Phillip Island and that cemented our feelings for each other; we stayed in bed practically all the time. Mark told me about his family, saying that they were pretty cool but they didn't like him having girlfriends who weren't Greek.

I wasn't particularly interested in his parents anyway. My working visa was crawling away to its end and I had no idea how I was going to stay in the country. I called up a few introduction agencies hoping they could set me up with someone. Then I met a client at work who'd just lost his job and who seemed interested when I joked that I wanted to pay someone to help me stay in the country. He looked like Elvis Presley except for his huge nose. He told me he'd always wanted a nose job and with the money I'd give him he'd get it fixed. It seemed a fair exchange: a nose job for residency. But then he backed out at the last minute. Then there was another client who was willing but when I thought about it, I couldn't bear the thought of sharing the same roof with someone I hardly knew. So at the end of the day stood Mark, who was kind and considerate and I'd known him for a while now, and everything about him seemed good. He didn't know that I was working, and I was sure that if I told him he wouldn't want to know me. I didn't want to stop working because it was all I knew, and besides, it was what I had been doing when I met him. So I lied.

It wasn't difficult. I asked him to call me in the late afternoon, just as I was getting ready to go to work. I said I couldn't give him my work number because my boss didn't like the staff to have personal phone calls. He thought I was very innocent anyway, because I was very quiet with him. In fact during the whole time I knew him I would have said very little. He would always take me along to his friends' twenty-first parties and he would do all the talking while I would just stand there like a dummy.

Mark must have appreciated my silent ways because one night, when we'd just come back from his favourite pizza place, he said he didn't want to see me go back to England, that he wanted me to stay. He said he'd thought about it, and he'd sponsor me as a de facto and just say nothing about it while he was living at home. It seemed a long shot because we could easily have been found out, and after all it was fraud, lying to the government. But Mark wasn't afraid of the government and neither was I, particularly. So we got the application forms, I got a flat in Balwyn and we filled out the forms saying we were living as de factos. It was as easy as that. I gave up my job at Decadence and got a job in a day brothel and things went on much the same except that now I had a chance of getting residency, without worrying who, when and how. I was just lucky that my boyfriend wanted to sponsor me into the country.

The day job was at Lovely Ladies. It was owned by an Arabic man who had a bad reputation as a pimp and a sleaze, but I'd heard it was the busiest day place in Melbourne. It had the most girls and the most clients.

Going in to look around, I was greeted by Ted, the owner, who said in a very polite voice, 'Hello, how are you?' It didn't suit his image, a man in his forties who had dark brooding eyes, wrinkly orange skin and a hooked nose. He was six foot with blow-waved black hair brushed back off his face in a pimp style. He was wearing leather pants and his shirt undone to his chest to show off his gold chains and hairy chest. He looked too much like a cliché to be taken that seriously. He looked as if he must have been watching Taxi Driver a few times before he decided to pimp women.

He showed me around the double-story town house that had young girls coming out of everywhere. It was a middle-sized brothel with six rooms. The rooms were simple and everything smelt dusty, and the place looked as if it needed a change in bed sheets. There were showers in

most of the rooms and the other ones had communal showers. Downstairs they had the reception area and lounge,
where the girls and clients sat together on the couches.
Most of the clients were Asians who couldn't speak much
English, but there was no need to be sociable at all. It was
a relaxed atmosphere and although there was no television to stare at, they were playing CDs and there were the
usual magazine table spreads.

Ted wanted me to do a few clients straight away, since I
was already here. He said he would guarantee me five hundred in four hours. There were a lot of clients sitting
around but I thought I would wait until the following day.
So I left.

Ted was right; I could make five hundred dollars quickly.
I went into work in the morning and got ready in a simple
white dress that showed off my legs and pale skin, and
started getting client after client. Ted got me most of the
bookings. The clients all wanted to see new girls and the
Asians wanted to see new and young girls, so I knew I
would do well. Ted would pull the clients aside as they
came in and say, 'This one's new and gives good service',
and then he'd grab my arm and push me towards the client and tell me to take him to a room.

The Asian clients came very quickly and I would have a
hostess knocking on the door within ten minutes of the
booking, ready with the next one. Eighty five dollars was
spent very quickly but they didn't seem to mind; in fact
they found it quite funny that they could be ripped off so
badly with regard to time. All the clients knew Ted and
most liked him. They all thought he looked after them by
giving them the best girls and the new girls they craved

for.

The other working girls were jealous that I got all the bookings but that was standard with anyone new. They would get over it in a week. The receptionist, Christine, was nice. She looked like Madonna. She would sit all day long at reception answering the phone and fixing her hair and make-up. One of the girls said Ted was fucking her. She'd worked before, for a long time, since she was fourteen. She'd stopped recently and now just did reception work, and saw clients only when she needed extra money.

There were quite a few girls who had worked there for a while. It was a very casual brothel; there were no shifts. Ted opened up at around ten in the morning and closed at eight at night and the girls could drop in and leave any time they wanted. He was obviously a very shrewd business man to give working girls such flexibility. It meant he had the most girls, and the most beautiful girls, working at his place.

He would always advertise for hostesses and then once they'd started he'd try to get them to work in the rooms. The clients loved the new flesh walking around and it was good for business, even if they didn't end up working in the rooms. Sometimes there were more hostesses than girls actually working, and these girls were offered thousands of dollars by clients to sleep with them. I suppose it was a game to the clients, tempting the hostesses with vast amounts of money.

All the girls were sleazed on by Ted. He'd try and get all the new ones into bed. In Melbourne girls almost never did bookings with owners but no-one had told Ted that. He was notorious for trying to get a head job off a girl before she started. If she hadn't worked before she wouldn't have known any better, so usually it was Ted who got in with the first head job, not the clients.

Ted did have a sense of humour though, and he was very funny at times. He had a way of sneering at all the girls, especially Christine, that was just hilarious. His favourite saying was, 'Stick with me baby and you'll have diamonds'. Yet he wore the same clothes day in and day out and only smelt okay because he always wore expensive aftershave. Everyone had heard a rumour about Ted. Some said he had AIDS from sleeping with all the working girls. And others said he was kinky and that he liked to bash girls and piss and shit on them.

I knew he used speed most days to keep going. How else can someone work all the time — he took girls back to his place and worked there as well — and not get tired? He liked young girls and I knew that he had found Christine on the street when she was a kid, and took her in and looked after her, but all the time he was video-taping her having sex with him and selling it overseas. She found out about this from a working girl so he started paying her one hundred dollars a week to keep her mouth shut.

In the first month I'd made and saved a lot of money. I was working all day, five days a week and seeing about six clients a day. Most of them became my regulars because I still worked hard in the room. It was tiring after a while to have to devote so much energy to making sure the client had a great time, and then doing it again and again. But watching the girls who'd worked for a long time sit around and do nothing was depressing too. They would moan at Ted about how they needed money for rent and this and that and Ted would try and get them bookings. It sounded desperate. For the time being I was lucky that I didn't have too many empty hours on my hands. Sitting around doing nothing was so boring, I could quite easily understand why so many of the girls took drugs.

A few were working solely to support their drug habit. Ted hated these girls and had no respect for them but he still let them work. If a girl had been a junkie it was like having a huge mark against her name. These girls really had problems. Some of them would get into a pretty bad state at work. They would be falling asleep on the couches and collapsing on the ground. Sometimes they would shoot up before they came to work or otherwise they would go into the old empty terrace house next door and shoot up there. Because I hadn't touched drugs, I couldn't imagine how they felt. Sometimes I felt sorry for them and the mess that they had got themselves into. My brother had been a junkie in England before I'd left and I'd seen what his drug habit had done to his life, and to my mother's and mine.

I would dread it when he was home; I knew it would be the beginning of another nightmare. When I'd come back from school he'd be hanging around home, hassling mum to lend him some money when she got home from work, and freaking out if she wouldn't. I suppose he needed it for another hit, but she didn't know then. He'd changed a lot since he'd been working away from home. He'd had his hair cut into a mohican style — it made him look sinister and I suppose he was living out that fantasy with his friends. One of them was one I'd known since primary school and I could feel his eyes all over me. He reminded me of the many times he and my brother had their hands on my body when mum thought we were out playing together. Somehow they made me feel dirty.

Other times he'd be at home by himself, watching TV, out of it after a hit or bottles of booze, and he'd just piss on the carpet without so much as a care, because he didn't even know what he was doing.

Chapter 6

Out for Lunch

Christmas was drawing near again and Mark hadn't told his family that I was still in the country. They knew he'd been seeing me, but they thought I was long gone. Unfortunately I had to spend that Christmas alone because he had to be with his family. While it was happy in one way — I was still in Australia and it looked as if I was going to get what I wanted — I felt sadder and lonlier than ever. I even thought of what it would be like if I killed myself. I knew I didn't have the guts to do it, but it was comforting just playing around with the idea of ending my misery.

Mark came over on Boxing Day and I cooked and things didn't seem that bad. We planned on taking a holiday in Surfers Paradise in January, during his long vacation. It would be nice to get away, and I needed a break from the clients too. Work had once again settled into a routine. It turned out that Ted liked me and would always help me get lots of bookings. I was reliable, hard-working and I didn't touch drugs, and Ted was always wondering when I would give in and go out to dinner with him. He kept asking and I thought he must have been joking — I wouldn't have touched him with a barge pole.

I had got used to the girls working there and they became my security. I felt a comradeship with them, because it was a tough job and I was doing it alongside them. Some of them were my friends, but I wasn't close to any of them; there was a certain amount of bitchiness amongst them and there was jealousy in how many bookings you got or what you got up to in the rooms.

Outside the brothel I felt I was different from everyone else because I was a prostitute. I thought I was smart keeping it from my boyfriend, but I was still very unhappy about working there. I thought there must be something wrong with me and my family had always said that I was weird and too quiet. I hadn't changed that much: I felt I was still weird, but at least now I was beginning to talk more. I'd had an O.C.D., obsessional compulsive disorder, when I was young, checking everything a million times before I could get it out of my mind; was the cooker — or whatever it was that I was checking — turned off? In my teenage years, after I'd become more relaxed, the problem just disappeared. I'd always felt confused about why I had been like that and I read later that it was more a hiccup in the brain chemistry than anything psychological. I think stress played a major part in it, because since I'd been working in brothels, the problem had come back, and it seemed to me that once more I was a victim of my own mind.

Working as a hooker had restored some of my self-confidence; it had made me feel better about my looks, which I'd always hated. I had become more at ease with my body, and taking my clothes off was no big deal any more. I was still shy and I was certainly no extrovert, even though I would have loved to be, but I thought I just didn't quite have it. Other working girls I'd noticed were always talking and laughing and looking as if they were at least involved in something. I felt involved in nothing and my only escape, when I was waiting for the clients, was in to magazines and books. Clients would watch me as I brooded my way through words.

I started doing more double bookings since Ted had a special going in the lunch hour: two girls together for the price of one. It would bring new customers in for such a great offer, but then he would start charging them the real prices. I still hated doing double bookings. On occasions I would enjoy it if the girl was nice, but usually the guy would get so excited he would want to fuck every hole he saw, so there were many condom changes going from girl to girl. I was never turned on by any of it — in fact I used to think it was boring. For me watching a client fuck someone was about as exciting as watching paint dry. Usually we would make faces at each other and try and get the guy off as quickly as possible. I never did bi-twins but that was another of Ted's specialities that he had going.

Out for lunch

The Asian clients were my bread and butter. They loved my pale skin and natural looks. Most of them were from Vietnam and Hong Kong, and couldn't speak English very well, so they would always come to Ted (he spoke Chinese) because they trusted him. The prices were reasonable, so all the girls were affordable, and young and pretty. The Asian clients were the easiest because they were quick and non-sleazy, and most of them wanted to come twice in half an hour, and that always meant an extra twenty dollars. It could be tiring having sex twice in half an hour but their cocks weren't as big as Westerners so it meant you didn't get so sore.

I had my fair share of nasty clients, who were usually Arabic. They could be really rough in the room. They had a habit of biting hard on body parts and pulling your body around on the bed, like a piece of meat. I used to think that they must have just hated hookers.

The Turks always shaved their pubic hair for hygienic reasons and I alway thought it made their cocks look odd. Somehow their bodies didn't seem that sexy; the lack of hair took the animal effect away. It was the same for girls who shaved all their pussies: it looked really unsexy.

Usually the worst clients were the young kids who would sometimes come in for a dare. They were usually the biggest pain in the butt, and it was always a big deal for them to fuck a hooker. They thought they were being really bad, and you could see them thinking, if only mum could see me now. They would always come in together for moral support, usually in groups of two or three. They looked around sixteen or seventeen. It was Ted's job to ask for I.D., but he never did unless they looked younger than his under-age girls. Some of the boys were virgins, who'd come to lose their virginity here. It was awkward with them, because they didn't know what to do and it was like being their schoolteacher. They'd nervously fumble their way around the bed with an instant hard-on and not much idea of foreplay. Their bodies looked so boyish; I never really found it much of a turn-on, although some of the girls in other brothels I knew craved these young virgins. They'd come in about two seconds, with a few uncoordinated thrusts and it would be all over. I made an effort to make it special for them, but really they were just another client. Other young guys, however, were really hard work, because they had a lot of energy and they'd just want to keep having sex and coming until it was time for them to leave. Most of them were fascinated at how I could sleep with men twice my age, and they wanted to know why I worked. It was the money, I always told them.

There were quite a few clients who took drugs, always Ted's friends. They were like dirty leeches hanging around at night-time. I saw a few of them, but I was too straight for most of them. They were always looking for little extras like oral sex without a condom. And they never paid; it was always on the house.

I did one escort booking with a regular who was a known speed user. He always booked himself into hotels and got girls to come out to him. I was called half-way through a booking he'd been doing with another girl, and they wanted me to join them. I was really nervous because the girl had mentioned that he wanted to see two girls together. By the time I got there they were in the bath together. Suzy, who'd worked for a few years, had a great body and huge breasts, and as I got undressed in the other room and then climbed into the tub I felt embarrassed about my body. We sat there talking and it looked as if Peter was speeding off his face. He kept licking his lips like a crazy, thirsty snake. Suzy offered to shave my pussy because Peter preferred his pussies neat and easy to lick. I declined her offer since I had always liked mine *au naturel.*

When we had finished in the tub, we sat around on the bed and Peter pulled out a huge bag of white powder. I'd whispered to Suzy, while we were drying off, that I didn't want any drugs but she said a bit wouldn't hurt, and it would help us get into the booking. I sort of trusted her — after all she looked fine. So Peter tipped speed into our drinks and we drank.

Almost immediately everything speeded up and was more exciting. Suzy was pulling Peter's cock, which was pretty small, but it looked more exciting than before. Peter had my legs open looking at my cunt. He kept on asking me to show him my cunt over and over again. Suzy started kissing my nipples and putting her fingers inside me. She seemed to like my body and I liked hers too.

Peter was into quite a few things. He liked anal sex and he got Suzy to stick her hand up his arse — with a glove — and fuck him like that. I was amazed she got her whole hand in there. Then he wanted to be fucked by a drinking glass. As Suzy pushed it in and out of him, I was terrified it was going to break inside him. Things got even more bizarre when he wanted to be blind-folded and we laid him on the couch and took turns sitting on his face. He then wanted us to do a golden shower and piss all over him, and in his mouth, while he pulled his cock, and with deep heat all over his balls. When he asked us to put the deep heat on his balls, I thought he said put it on his cock, so he got a rather nasty surprise — the deep-heat must have gone up the eye of his penis and burnt him. In the grand finale, when he was meant to come heaps after all those drugs and kinky sex, he didn't, because he was in too much pain.

Needless to say he never again wanted to do a booking with me. I went home looking as if I had done a stack of drugs, and couldn't sleep until the next morning.

In the middle of January Mark and I went on our holiday to Surfers Paradise as planned. It was a good break and I needed the rest. I realised, as you often do when you go on holidays with boyfriends, that there were lots of differences between us. I hadn't shared the same bed with him for more than two days running — he was still living with his parents — and after a week I really felt the strain of being with him. I began to feel glad that he lived at his parents' place.

Coming back from Surfers', he got sick from an infection he'd picked up and while I was at work ended up in hospital. When I came home his sister was waiting for me to take me there. She still lived at home but she hated her parents. I knew that they had been trying to marry her off to a Greek husband since she was sixteen, but she had gone her own way and studied art at university and then teaching.

When I walked in, I saw Mark lying on the hospital bed with a drip in his arm and he looked very sick. His mum and dad were sitting next to him, his mum with a pained look on her face and his dad looking as if he could be reading a newspaper. I kissed Mark on the forehead and hugged him as his mum looked away in disgust. They had dragged it out of him that he'd been lying to them the whole time, and he'd been seeing me and not a nice Greek girl, as he was supposed to be. They'd been shocked to find out that he'd been in Surfers Paradise with me, and not his friends. Now the truth was out and I could see the contempt in their eyes.

I tried not to notice the long silence as I walked out with his sister. I waved Mark goodbye and smiled at his parents who scowled back at me.

The next day he was fine and fully recovered, back at his parents' place. But things had taken a dive; they had forbidden him to see me, and they were spying on him to make sure he was nowhere near me. Luckily they didn't know where I lived.

Mark eventually cracked under the pressure of living with over-bearing parents and decided to move in with me. It seemed a good idea: I wouldn't have to worry about the interview at immigration because this time we really would be living together as de factos. I also thought it would be a nice change to have someone with me at home, instead of being alone all the time — I conveniently forgot what it had been like in Surfers.

Mark moved out of home while his parents were at work and left a note saying that he wasn't coming back, so they'd leave him alone. I doubted this as I watched him move his belongings from his car into my place.

I was right; in a matter of days they had somehow

traced where I was living, and were banging on the door while I was at work. He was in a bad state when I got back; more than anything he felt as if his parents were terrorising him. I was glad now that he'd defied them, and was living with me. Obviously they had under-estimated his strength. He hadn't even let his mum in even after she'd been banging on the door for hours. Then his uncle came and, one by one, practically his entire family. If he'd gone back then I doubt whether he would have seen me again. They probably would have locked him up in his room.

After a few weeks we settled into a routine of work, home, and boyfriend/girlfriend things. Mark wanted to settle down and start looking for a house. He might as well have been talking to me in a foreign language. I felt very unsettled and the last thing I wanted was a loan on an A.V. Jennings house. Then out of the blue, when we were driving back from looking at matchbox houses and talking about how he wanted to get Austudy and how he could only get it if he was married, he said how about it — do you want to get married then? I guess it could have had something to do with immigration or maybe with defying his parents again, but we decided to get married.

We did it for all the wrong reasons and after a few short moments at a registry office, it didn't feel like we were married anyway.

Dressed in a white cotton suit, with make-up and my long hair curled, we took our vows before a few of Mark's uni friends. I couldn't really invite anyone from work, because I was sure one of the girls would let something slip. Tim, the best man, and Mark's old school friend, had picked us up in his car and driven us there. He'd handed

Mark the emerald ring which Mark had bought for me. He slipped it on my finger, we said our stuff, kissed and that was it.

We didn't have a reception, instead we went out for a celebrationary dinner, although there really wasn't much to celebrate. I felt ridiculous about everything. I was only marrying him to get my residency and he, because he wanted me and Austudy in the process, but we pretended to each other that we were doing it, because we were in love. I wondered what his friends thought about it all. The whole thing was wrong. At the restaurant, as everyone sat around talking and drinking, I watched the sky turn to dusk outside and I felt so sad about everything. There was no romance, there was no mystery, as we headed back to our flat .

Somehow, being married made me feel trapped and I hated every second of it. Mark said I had changed from being nice to being a bitch. I suppose at the back of my mind was the thought that I had secured residency, so now there was no longer the need to try. I had no intention of staying married. I couldn't get used to the idea of a life that was go to work, come home, cook, have sex, pay the bills, have a few kids, mow the lawns and so on and so on, as he obviously intended. I just wanted to be free to do what I wanted.

Whatever I might have thought about marriage, I suffered incredible guilt from working as a prostitute behind Mark's back. At times I felt I was being just so smart and at other times I felt bad about lying to him, now that we were married. But I never gave up work because it was just so easy to go into Ted's. I knew him, I knew the girls, and then there was the money; there was everything that made me feel secure. Mark didn't make me feel one bit secure, and he wasn't contributing towards any of the bills, so I just carried on. He was studying at university full-time, and since he wasn't working at his parents' business anymore, he didn't have any money, except Austudy, which he was trying to save for our future. Most of the time I'd come home from work, tired, and he would be back from university, playing on his computer. He'd say something like 'Hi honey, what's for dinner?' And the whole night would pass with me just being a sucker and waiting on and cleaning up after him. He expected nothing less; his mother had done it for him so why shouldn't his wife do the same?

Time passed like this, with a few dramas in between from his parents, who were less than thrilled to know that their only son had married behind their backs and they hadn't even been invited to the wedding.

Then came the day that I seemed to have been waiting for forever: the interview for residency. Mark panicked and messed up the entire thing, and, under the pressure of the questions, almost confessed to everything we had done. Fortunately, my in-laws knew some people who worked in Immigration and, even after everything that had happened, they were the ones who got me residency. Their strategy, as I was to find out later, was: give the bitch what she wants and she'll leave our son alone. Unfortunately, they had it all wrong, but one thing was for sure — I felt I was on top of the world the day I got my residency.

I was still working at Ted's, and now I was one of the old girls. Even though I'd worked for so long, I only had about ten thousand dollars saved, which I had stashed away in a security deposit box. Some of the old regulars still stuck by me, but there were only a few. There was the old guy who went to the Philippines on a regular basis to see young girls. He would tell me how he paid money to the parents of nine-year-old girls to fuck their daughters. I found him disgusting, but back then it was better than not having fifty dollars. He would lick his lips and talk in a raspy voice about how tight their pussies were, and how they didn't even have breasts yet. The only reason he liked to see me was because I could still pass for a teenager, even if I was past his ideal age of nine.

Most of the Asian clients were totally unfaithful and would only see the new girls, but a few still liked me and saw me on a regular basis. It was beginning to look as if my time had run out; I had been here too long. I was now twenty-two and too old for this place.

Now that I had residency, I didn't have to worry about whether Mark found out I was a prostitute, and I reasoned that I could go back to working nights and earning lots of money again. I had found out about a place just outside the city that a girl had said was really busy, and I was ready for a change.

Chapter 7

Lost

It was opposite a park, a run-down, grey looking terrace, with two other brothels, all standing in a row. Even though it was bright outside, inside it was dark. I sat there with the other working girls in the lounge-room, waiting for the receptionist to finish on the phone. One of the girls nodded enthusiastically towards me and I smiled back. I recognised her from another brothel, but I wasn't sure which one.

The receptionist said there was a space on the roster on Thursday if I wanted to start. She asked me what name I wanted to use. I thought about it for a while. I'd changed my name so many times since I started work. I'd been

Samantha, Cathy, Sarah, and now I thought I needed a change of image. I decided on Sasha.

When I got home, I told Mark that I wanted to start saving some money for a house. And then a week later I told him that I'd got a job cleaning offices and banks at night, to cover why I'd be working until five and six in the morning. He believed me. He'd asked once or twice about work in general, but I always made out my job was boring, so I never talked about it.

Our relationship had been getting gradually worse as time went on. He'd failed some of his exams and consequently had to repeat the subjects he'd failed. His parents had been back-stabbing me to his relatives and I think it just added to the pressure of everything. We'd stopped going over to their place for their little dinner get-togethers, which was just as well, because I hated them. It was obvious they didn't trust me. They'd make a point of closing all the doors in the house in case I stole something, yet they insisted I call them mum and dad. At first the things they did hurt, but in the end I just didn't care.

At least now I was working nights there would be no more worries about Mark wanting phone numbers.

Working at the Meeting Place was exactly what I needed. I'd been trying to save money for years at Ted's but it wasn't busy enough. At least here I could work really hard for one year, and have enough to buy a house. Buying a house became an obsession for me. I wanted something to show for working; I didn't want all these years wasted on nothing. I blamed Mark for wasting so much of my time when I could have been hard at it. I couldn't wait now for him to leave; in fact I was thinking of soon leaving him. I just needed a few more months after getting residency, so it wouldn't look too suspicious.

On the first night I started working at the Meeting Place I saw seven clients and made over four hundred dollars. I was told that it was a quiet night, and the weekends were busier. I was instantly drawn to working there; I felt very much at home. Most of the girls there were addicted to drugs and they worked to pay for their habits. There were some straight girls as well, working to save for a house, or working just because the money alone was so great.

The girls were really funny, out of it or not; they made good company and I actually felt that I had come home to myself. The place in itself was becoming an addiction and I looked forward to working there, even more than going out to a club; it was more fun, and, more important to me, I got to make money.

I was hardly seeing anything of Mark. He was studying hard for his final year and had also gone back to work for his parents. On my nights off, I hardly felt like his company, but he did try to make an effort and in fact he'd cook for me sometimes and leave it in the microwave for when I got home, hungry in the morning.

Most brothels I'd worked in before were boring — the girls always took themselves and their drug problems too seriously. But here there were no rules. The girls were allowed to smoke joints and shoot up, as long as they kept making the house money. They hardly hid their drug problems; it was always a big rush at around eight o'clock at night when everyone turned up late for work, to find out who they could score from, and who had the best stuff.

One girl, Tracy, used to deal mainly to the rest of the

girls, when their boyfriends couldn't score for them. I remember the first night she walked in, all bushy blonde hair and chubby cheeks. She looked about thirty-five and had an over-weight pale body and one of those faces that look like a Cabbage Patch doll. She seemed to be on a different planet from the look on her face. I noticed she made eye contact with a few of the girls who had been fidgeting nervously for a while.

Because I was new I was given the cold treatment for a few days, and then gradually as they got used to me, I became one of them. I got a reputation for being a square, because this was mainly a drug haunt, but I think some of them might have actually liked me for that. I was the youngest one working there, and I got the most bookings in the beginning. The ages ranged up to sixty, with most in their late twenties and early thirties. Some had worked for as long as ten years, and others longer. They all had one thing in common, and that was they all liked the money there.

We would do our introductions in a long corridor and the clients would stand waiting for the girls to come out and talk to them. Here, if you wanted to get a booking you'd have to work for it, or else someone else would get the client. You had to go into lengthy detail about what you'd actually do in the room. For a straight service it was seventy dollars — the house would get thirty — and they'd just get a massage and straight sex. Then the prices went up for kissing, oral sex which some girls did without a condom — anal sex, fantasies, fetishes. Sometimes girls would specialise in something like bondage or submissive, but just about everyone would do something for extra money. Otherwise you could end up doing forty dollar bookings all night, earning little and going home with a sore pussy.

My sex life with Mark had died to virtually nothing. I never felt like having sex with him and when he'd get upset and complain and say that I never wanted to do it, I'd let him, just to shut him up. I'd lay there, unfeeling and cold towards him, telling him to hurry up and come. My attitude towards him changed and I began to dislike him almost as much as I disliked his family, maybe because I blamed him for making me hide what I was doing.

I was really shy talking to the clients and I'd say my introduction as fast as possible. I never had smart comebacks as the other girls did for rude clients. I did a lot of straight bookings in the beginning, but the older girls warned me not to wear out my body while I was young. Some of them had worked for so long they'd lost control of their bladders, and they'd piss themselves on the couches without even knowing.

Some girls would do just about anything in the room for enough money. I'd heard stories of a client who used to bring his dog in, and get one of the girls to have oral sex with the poor thing, while he pulled himself watching. Apparently the Meeting Place had been pretty wild about ten years before, when just about anything went. One of the girls told me a story of a gorgeous young girl who had come to work there and got all the bookings. All of the other girls had become jealous of her looks and the clients she got, so one girl tricked her into doing a submissive booking with her and a client who was into heavy bondage. Once she was tied up and gagged in the room, they both whipped her badly and burnt her with cigarette butts. Apparently she was scarred for life and no-one could blame the client, since she'd agreed to do the booking, and that is what he wanted to do. She went out screaming and never came back.

Now the place was a litttle tamer and most of the girls who had worked back then were either dead or burnt out from smack. Tracy was one of the few who remained and was still going strong, and the bondage lady who told me that story was still there, but apart from a few others, that was about it.

The clients varied greatly depending on the night. They were not as nice as in the other brothels but they were used to paying extra money for what they wanted. The weekend was the busiest and best because all the young Greeks and Italians would come through from the nightclubs. They would always be loud and drunk, but most of them were good-looking and it was better fucking them than some jerk-off business client. Sometimes I really used to like the sex; most of them here did. I liked doing fantasies and dressing up — usually most guys would choose a schoolgirl, and I would go into the booking dressed in a school-dress, stockings and suspenders.

It would be easy to act out a scene and bring the client into it, and they really got off on it. The Meeting Place advertised doing fantasies and catering for fetishes, and there would always be one girl able to do what they wanted. I would only do light bondage to guys but I always used to get a little nervous when I was doing it. Dominating and whipping never really did anything for me.

I did one submissive booking with a Japanese client who wanted a girl to dominate. It turned out to be quite bizarre. When I went into the room I thought he would have only wanted to whip me lightly, as we had discussed earlier, but on the bed he had all kinds off different whips laid out. He'd paid me three hundred dollars for an hour, so I didn't want to back out, but when he took his clothes off, his body was covered in deep red gashes! I knew beforehand that he liked bondage on him as well, but I didn't know he liked that much of it. I was nervous and already sweating quite heavily when he tied me up on the bed, naked. I made sure I could get out of the knots he'd tied my hands in. When he was whipping me, and he did it very lightly, I felt quite scared because I knew he was really into it.

He wanted to drip hot candle wax onto my body but I refused, so then he suggested tying me up from the hanging rack, which they had suspended on the ceiling, but I refused again. He became very frustrated with the booking because there wasn't much I would do. So he got me to whip him instead. I felt queasy about whipping his body already covered from head to toe in deep gashes.

When my hour was up it was time for him to be tortured professionally by Maddy, the full-time bondage lady. She suspended him from the ceiling, gagged him, stuck a huge dildo up his arse, rubbed deep heat into his balls, teased him with a knife around his cock and then proceeded to whip him really hard. I watched for a while in amazement, marvelling at how any one could get off on that much pain. His face looked as though he was in agony, but his cock was hard. And after all that Maddy got him to take a red hot shower to soothe his pain!

As I became more familiar with the Meeting Place I started experimenting in different bookings. I did anal sex a few times because I could get so much more money for it. At first I practiced with my husband, at home, which spiced up our otherwise dead sex-life. However I found it hard to relax, and when a cock was too big it ended up being very painful. But usually a client would put it in for one minute and he'd come anyway.

I got into doing a lot of golden showers, which is when you get to drink five glasses of water before a booking and then go and piss it all over the client. In the end I quite liked it, and I could make myself come as I pissed into the client's mouth. The clients would lick the piss and come from my cunt as if they couldn't get enough. My favourite was doing it when I was dressed in a school uniform. So many clients requested a golden shower that it seemed the place was going through a trend of pissing.

Heaps of clients liked their anus penetrated. My vibrator was in constant use in and out of men's bottoms. I also had a locker full of lingerie that I changed into for seductive bookings, but from night to night I usually wore very tight, clingy outfits that would show off my skinny body and long legs. Usually one outfit would work better than the other and there would always be one dress that the clients loved, and you would make heaps of money in it.

The late nights were once again very tiring. Most girls kept awake with drugs, but I only had coffees — I was more interested in saving money. It seemed the girls who used drugs were always in some kind of mess with themselves or more often with their boyfriends. I felt sorry for them, but envious sometimes of their carefree attitude to life. I would always ask the girls who used smack whether they regretted it, and they always did. Some were on programs to get off the drugs but there weren't many of these back then. A few said they wouldn't have a life without drugs. But to me they were the same people whether they took drugs or not.

I was amazed how some had survived so long on drugs but, as I found out, heroin is the one that you can survive longer on than any other. The new girls always used speed. Most would snort it but a few would shoot it as well. To them it was like having a short black coffee.

Clients rarely offered me drugs in the room, except on one occasion when I saw a client who had some cocaine. He offered me a few lines, and I'd never snorted drugs before, so I wasn't sure how to do it. Somehow I managed to blow it all into the air instead of snorting it into my nose. It was very embarassing and the client wasn't very impressed, although he found it quite amusing. He showed me how to put it on the inside of my gums and feel the effect that way. It didn't really do much for me, other than making me feel more awake and excited than before. I felt better in that I didn't feel bored any more, but doing coke and having great sex was not as wonderful as all the other girls had made it out to be, (or maybe it was bad coke, and he was a bad fuck).

I still had my own natural excitement from being naughty and working in a seedy environment, and earning a lot of money. But all that was about to change when my health took a dive. I was in a booking in one of the rooms upstairs, and I'd been through the usual routine of sucking the client's dick and then having sex, when he told me at the end of the booking that he'd seen a bald spot at the back of my head. Afterwards, when I went down into the girls' room and saw for myself in the mirror, he was right — I had a bald spot on the right side of my head, at the back, about the size of a twenty-cent coin.

One of the girls came in and told me it looked like I had alopecia. She'd known someone who'd had it before, and it was brought on by stress. I didn't feel I was stressed out, but I'd put my body through months of long nights and endless bookings.

I went home in tears at three in the morning. I knew it was only hair, but it was my hair and it was a shock, just losing it like that. I never really felt the same about working at the Meeting Place after that. I didn't enjoy it as I used to, because I was alway wary of my hair falling out, and of clients noticing the hair that had already fallen out. At home, every time I vacuumed I noticed hundreds of hairs everywhere. The alopecia got worse and I stopped work.

One night when I was lying in bed sick from depression and flu I started an argument that I had every intention of using to finish our marriage. It had never been a real marriage, I thought, lying there, waiting for Mark to come back from the corner shop.

Our marriage had been one more of circumstance and convenience. I'd lied to him and myself that it was going to work. There hadn't seemed much chance of it ever succeeding whilst I was working behind his back in a brothel the entire time. We did have hopes when we first got married, but as time went on, it was obvious to me that it was never going to work. I became more interested in making my own plans, of providing my own security.

Mark had other ideas. He thought we were going to be together for the rest of our lives, but I couldn't see that happening. I'd grown sick of him in the early days of our marriage and now we didn't have anything left to say to each other — there was no passion and no spark. It didn't seem to bother Mark, however: he obviously thought boredom was normal. He obviously thought we would stay married forever and grow old together, as his parents had, bitter and twisted. Only recently we'd been fighting over when I should have children, which he expected me to start churning out in a few years. I just couldn't come round to his way of thinking, and besides, his attitude that it was my duty to cook and clean was beginning to get to me.

We weren't suited, and I wasn't in the mood to bullshit any more. So when he came back from the shop, I told him how he was causing my alopecia. He and his parents were constantly on my back about something or another, and now I'd had enough. I told him that I didn't want to buy a house, I never had any intention of having children and that we'd be better off apart.

My heart hurt as his eyes searched for some hint of a reason. But I had gone past the point of no return and now there was nothing for him to do but pack his stuff and get out. It would be easier that way.

He tried to make me come round and see reason, but I was in a black mood and I'd come to the end of it all: I just couldn't keep this charade going anymore, it was making me sick. He'd seen for himself that we'd been fighting more and not getting along in the past few months, so if leaving me was what it took to make me happy, then that's what he'd do.

So he called his parents to let them know he was coming home, and that he needed the van to take his stuff. He didn't really sound bitter or upset; he just sounded like a man going through all the sadness of leaving.

I lay in bed under the covers, feeling a flood of emotion and sorrow for everything I'd done. I was the one who was bitter and twisted. How could I trick my husband and treat him like this after all that we'd been to each other? I did love him as much as I knew how to. Even though I'd lied the whole time, I couldn't help but feel some emotion for the someone who'd shared my life for the last two and a half years. We'd been friends at best and he'd never tried to hurt me.

When he came back with the van from his parents' place, I thought I was dying inside. I lay on the bed, crying, and wishing I hadn't said the things I had. I didn't want him to go; I wanted him to stay with his arms around me, comforting me and holding me. What had I done? What was I going to do? Now the money didn't seem worth it: I would have given up all the money I'd earned, and could earn, to have him back. But I couldn't bring myself to say the words; I couldn't stop him. It was too late. When he had finished packing, he came and stood by the side of my bed and looked at me for a long time. Then he said he'd always loved me and he always would.

He asked me if this was what I really wanted, for him to go like this.

I just looked away with sore eyes and tears spilling down on to the pillow. I wanted to say that I loved him too; that I still wanted him, that it had taken this for me to find out that I loved him. But I couldn't. I just lay there crying while he softly closed the door behind him.

Now that I was left alone in my own world, I was frightened. I didn't know what to do or what to think. How could I have allowed myself to be so confused? My heart ached so much that when I got up to go into the bathroom, I collapsed and crouched there in a ball, crying on the floor. I was so sorry for everthing that I had done. I kept on saying sorry over and over again, but there was no-one to hear. I'd got what I wanted, but now I had it I didn't want it any more.

I thought about calling Mark and talking to him, but when I dialled his parents' number, his mum told me to leave her son alone. I knew this was exactly what she'd been waiting for. She said I'd never see him again and that I wasn't ever to ring that number in the future. She was so cold. I never doubted her words.

I went back to bed, hoping to sleep off this daytime nightmare. The pain I felt was too much to bear; I would be better off unconcious. Maybe when I woke, I wouldn't feel so bad.

As soon as I woke however, sadness filled me. It felt like something squeezing my heart so tight I couldn't breathe. I guess after all those years I hadn't bargained on love getting in the way of what I wanted. In my own curled-up little world I felt more unloved than anyone I knew. My husband had said 'I love you' a thousand times, but it didn't mean a thing until he said it when he was leaving.

I knew I wasn't thinking straight. I was dangerously close to the edge, and I knew if I didn't talk to someone I would get worse. I had no friends I could call up and I was trapped inside my flat by my mind and my emotions. Alone, I felt the extent of my loneliness. I spent all day crying at home. The next day I called up the Meeting Place, the only friends and family I had.

I went into work, but I really only wanted the company and someone to talk to. Halfway through the night, I couldn't stand my own tangled-up emotions any more, and I went home in tears. I'd mentioned beforehand that I'd split up with my husband, but they hadn't even known I was married in the first place.

The next night I was working again, and I was a bit calmer. I told René, a girl I'd known for years from another brothel, and Lexy whom I'd met from working at the Meeting Place, and they were all truly sympathetic. They really got into the drama of it all, even though I knew I must have sounded a bit over the top, but for them it was an interesting diversion from work. I gave my side of the story, of how I was sick of my husband using me for money, and about his family who'd hated me from the start. I told them of how I'd been a slave to the kitchen until I started working here, and he hadn't helped with anything because he was spoilt. But when we'd split up I wasn't ready for the pain I felt. I told them I still loved him, but they said it wasn't love I felt, because how could I love someone like that? In a way I wanted them to talk me out of going back to him, because I knew I would. Maddie and Lexy said I needed a real man, not a wimp. They warned me if I did go back to him I'd have more problems with his family than I could cope with.

Mark had written me a letter a few days before, saying that it really was over, and that he wished me well for the future, but he didn't want to see me again. I couldn't leave it at that, so I kept leaving messages with his friends to call me. I wanted him back even though I had no idea what I would do when we were back together. Two weeks ago I had hated him and I couldn't wait to get rid of him; now I wanted him back again. I wasn't making sense, but I thought the right thing to do was to go with my heart.

Going to work was a kind of therapy. I would go in a mess and come out a mess, but the difference was, I felt less alone. The advice the girls gave me made more sense than I did, and they were the ones fucked up on drugs.

In the end Mark started missing me and began to come around. We kissed and made up, and he said he'd felt the same as I had, when he'd gone home that night. His parents really hated me and they didn't want him to see me, so he kept it a secret from them when he came around. It was like being back at the beginning again. But I was happy; I had got him back.

I'd saved about thirty thousand dollars working at the Meeting Place, and still had ten thousand from working at Ted's, and I was well on my way to getting what I wanted. But now I thought that getting a house meant nothing. It would just have been four walls: it might as well have been a coffin. I'd rather stay with my husband and be happy.

All the girls at work said I'd be stupid to go back with him, and I should have listened to them. I thought about going back home to England, to rest. I was so stressed out, and my hair was still falling out. I thought maybe a break would do me good and get me back on track . And then by chance, Mark was offered a job in Singapore. He'd graduated as an engineer during the entire drama, and one of his friends from university offered him a job at the same company where he was working. There wasn't much work for graduates in Melbourne, and it would be a good way for us to be together, well away from his parents.

So it was settled — I was going to England for a rest, and then I was going to join Mark in Singapore and we'd be back together again. I became more optimistic about my future, but I hadn't really thought things through properly. I was just drifting, hoping somehow things would work out. I'd more or less decided to give up work and concentrate on getting my health back, and that became my general goal. The more I worked the worse I seemed to become. If getting a house meant losing my hair then it wasn't worth the stress.

Chapter 8

Drifting

oing home was the next mistake I made. If I'd been looking for something back home, I might as well have headed off to Mars. It was good to see my mum again and it was nice being home, but nothing had changed in the years I'd been away. My mum had moved house but she still had the same furniture and decorations that brought back painful memories of the violence before I'd left. The arguments, the unhappy childhood and the abuse were etched in the bed that so many times I'd cried myself to sleep in.

My brother was living in Jersey, an island off the south coast of England, and he'd asked to see me, but I ranted and raved even at the mention of his name. I never wanted to see him again.

Before I'd left for Australia, he'd been working as a carpenter fitting out shops. He spent a lot of time working away from home , but he'd return on most weekends. I'd dread it when he was coming back because he'd always be arguing with my mother about something. Usually I tried to keep out of his way. Then one weekend when my mother was going through his suitcase for his washing she found a spoon, a dirty needle and one of his old ties with blood all over it. All the time my brother had been working away he'd been doing heroin, and no-one had known. That explained his rages and moods.

My brother confessed that he'd been using heroin for a couple of years. He said it had started when a workmate had offered him a fix and he'd taken it, because he said he wanted to be happy, instead of always being depressed about something. I knew that he had to work long hours to finish the jobs on time, and he was constantly living out of a suitcase. He'd been doing amateur cycling since he was young and he'd wanted to get into professional cycling, but didn't quite make the mark, and I think that stung him and took away his sense of direction.

When he started working away from home, at nineteen, he was easily led into fast fun, which was something he'd had no chance of when he was young. He'd missed lots of years from being in training all the time, and I suppose he had a lot of catching up to do.

Even though he had said he was going to give up heroin, he never did. When he had no work, he would spend weeks at home, usually in his room shooting up, and smoking dope and listening to music. I'd try and keep out of his way. He'd flown into a few rages over fights with mum about money and had smashed his hands into the doors, and once had thrown the telephone through the window when my mum tried to stop him calling his girlfriend long distance. My mum was scared of him too, but there was no-one around to stop my brother.

Often I would lie awake at night, frightened, when the local pub had closed, because I knew my brother would be coming back home to smash the house up. As he walked up the stairs he would start kicking his feet into the steps, smashing everything in his path. I was terrified he would hurt mum. It seemed he was blaming her for his miserable life, and all the boyfriends who had beaten him up. And he blamed her for our father's suicide. He kept on saying things about me, about why I was fucked up and that it was her fault.

This went on for ages. Mum couldn't cope with him and she would go and stay at her boyfriend's house, and I'd be left alone with him. I was eighteen at the time, but I'd stay in my room the entire time, too scared to come out. One night he came back drunk and stumbled into my room, leering at me. I pushed the door shut against him, terrified that maybe he'd rape me, and my old fears returned. But he'd drunk too much and could hardly stand up, so he left me alone.

He had a gun in his room that he'd used for shooting rabbits. Once he'd used a pellet to shoot me in the head, and I was frightened maybe next time it would be a real bullet. I had been sitting down watching TV and he was cleaning his gun and then when he'd finished, he loaded it and aimed it at my head. I yelled out to mum and tried to knock it away, but in the struggle, the gun went off and the air-gun pellet grazed the side of my head. The pain was excruciating, but I didn't want to give him the satisfaction of knowing how much he'd hurt me.

I knew he hated mum enough to kill her, and he was taking so many drugs that he was totally fucked up. Mum said he was exactly like his father and he even looked like him. I thought maybe he'd inherited the same mental disease.

Just before I went to Australia it got to the stage where I thought I was going crazy myself. I'd been abused from my childhood to what was happening to me now, and then seeing mum have a nervous breakdown, because she couldn't handle it, it all became too much for me. That was when I started working all the time to get enough money to escape from the nightmare.

Now it seemed I had come full circle. Being back in England made me realise that I hadn't exactly got very far. I had residency in Australia two and a half years after I arrived there, so I had a country to escape to, but I'd been through a lot to secure that, much more than I'd ever expected. Mum knew nothing about what had happened, but I never shared my feelings with her about anything, anyhow.

Being at home made me feel sick and my health actually got worse. I thought being in England would have lifted my spirits and that it would have been like the great homecoming — it was anything but. I called Mark in Singapore to let him know I was on my way. I made it sound like an adventure to myself and my family: my husband an engineer working abroad. I didn't want them to think I was a loser after all the years I'd been away. At least I had a smart husband.

I said goodbye to my family, and flew to Singapore. Mark met me at the airport, and took me back to the apartment he was sharing with his friend. It was very humid and I noticed that the city looked very neat. There was a lot of construction going on. After a few days, I felt quite settled; it was a welcome relief from England, which had been freezing cold. Mark and I were back together again and he had a contract to stay for up to a year.

Amazingly, after a week of bliss, I started getting calls from his parents, abusing and threatening me, just like old times. I could hardly believe it; everywhere Mark and I were together they somehow managed to find us. Their son was, after all, over eighteen and capable of looking after himself.

Mark somehow managed to lose his contract at work, something to do with him only just having graduated and not having enough experience and so we were forced to fly back to Melbourne after only two short weeks together.

His parents had been calling him in Singapore nearly every day since Mark had let slip that I was there with him, telling him to come back home and to 'get away from that slut'. They obviously hated me. As far as they were concerned, I was the wrong girl for their son. I even thought, that through a detective agency, maybe they'd discovered how I earned a living. Mark was scared of his parents and they had a great influence on him, so with no job to return to, he went back to his mother with his tail between his legs, and I moved into shared accommodation with a group of people in East St. Kilda.

I had never expected it to finish like that. My love for him, that I'd felt so strongly before, had died very quickly. As far as I was concerned, it was over. I couldn't love someone who wasn't prepared to stand up to his parents. He was too weak and I couldn't respect him for that.

So when he wanted to start seeing me again behind his parents' back, I told him we could only be friends. I felt nothing for him. I didn't want to have sex with him; he was beginning to turn me off. He suggested seeing a counsellor together, but I couldn't see the point; it was over.

Living in a huge house with a group of people was great. It took away my loneliness. We all got along well and everyone did their own thing. Some worked, others were on the dole, but everyone was very easy-going. Now I was with other people, I didn't miss Mark at all. I felt as free as a bird for the first time in my life.

I knew my husband was taking it very badly and had started seeing a psychiatrist. But for me, I began going out again and enjoying my freedom. Everyone at home smoked joints and they were always being passed around. I started going out for drinks and it felt good to be normal again, after all this time. I didn't feel like just a prostitute any more. I felt like a normal person.

It was around this time that I met Jordan. He seemed okay at first. He was nice, funny, charming, good-looking and great in bed. He had a small flat by himself in South Yarra and I used to go around to see him to smoke joints and have sex. He always had money and it seemed he never worked for it. He had a friend in prison who'd been arrested in possession of a gun. There were pictures of transsexuals around his flat, and he told me one had given him a head job.

He had pictures of other girls from when he worked for a modelling agency a few years before: it seemed Jordan was into eveything. He was skinny, with smooth pale skin and very prominent blue eyes; his other prominent feature was his huge cock. He was only twenty but he had had experience.

He could fuck for hours on end and I never got tired of it. I loved his cock, it was a nice change from Mark's, which was much smaller. He loved going down on me for hours and I remember having my first multiple orgasm after a few joints and valiums, with him between my legs.

But I should have been wary the first night I slept with him. Even though I was that drunk I was practically falling unconscious, I took a shower before we had sex, and I noticed he had one of those bathrooms that hints there is something wrong with a person. Everything was dirty, with old bits of soap and empty bottles everywhere, and there was not even a toilet roll.

When I went back into his room he insisted on playing Dead or Alive, which was his favourite group. He'd grown up in England and left when he was twelve. He was half Italian and half Irish. His parents separated when he was eighteen and he had a hard time dealing with it. Before that he'd had everything going for him. He'd cut a record and was looking forward to a recording career, but his parents' divorce affected him so badly he hit the bottle and started dealing dope and smoking a lot.

I was not a big dope-smoker myself. Often I would get dizzy if I had too much, and because I was fairly quiet the long silences really stood out. I would always laugh and muck around but smoking became more of an ordeal than anything. I always became very self-conscious on it and I could get quite paranoid. But the sex was good after a joint; I could really feel Jordan's cock inside me and he would do it for hours until I was so sore I couldn't do it any more. Then the pizza delivery guy would come and we'd eat pizza and drink cola.

I thought I was being pretty wild. I'd never met anyone like Jordan before. He was exciting to be around and because he was always very secretive about what he did, I found him mysterious. I thought maybe he was some kind of gangster. He was always disappearing, saying he had to be somewhere, and he knew guys who were in the Mafia — or so he said.

I thought I'd better go back to work. I'd had a long break and now it was time to make some money again. I didn't want to go hard at it like before; I never wanted to save money again, like before, and I never again wanted to work at the Meeting Place. I was quite happy working a few days just to get the money I needed to live. I had no definite plan for what I wanted to do. I just knew that I wanted to have some fun now that I was free. I didn't really care about a career, I just wanted to have fun and then die. Or preferably die having fun.

Going back to Ted's was the same as before, except this time I was a little bit more tired, and a little bit older. I was only twenty-three but there were at least ten other girls there that were younger-looking than me. I didn't look as good as before and I wasn't as enthusiastic; I'd lost it. I managed to get a few bookings here and there after sitting around for ages, but Ted would always feel sorry for me and try and give me money out of sympathy!

There were still a few of the old girls who had stuck it out after all these years. Most were working in other jobs part-time, and just came in when they needed the extra money. Some had taken time off to have children, and others were still battling the drugs. I would get bored working there. I still had about twenty thousand left in my security deposit but I wanted to keep that for emergencies.

I had my life on hold and I didn't know what to do. I felt I was different from how I'd been a few years ago. I had come out of myself more and I wasn't so closed in. I wanted to experience things and experiment; I didn't want to be so rigid or self-righteous. I wanted to enjoy my life. It always happens when life surprises you and turns you in a different direction.

By now, if I'd gone ahead with my original plans, I would still be working at the Meeting Place, and I'd be close to having earned a hundred thousand dollars. But that time between splitting up with my husband and the here and now had gone. I couldn't turn back the clocks and I wasn't about to go back.

Jordan was the perfect diversion. He was bad and he liked to have dare-devil fun. Mark had slipped into obscurity. It was over. He had no guts and he didn't interest me; I didn't care about him at all. He filed for divorce and I thought about taking him to court for his parents' money, because I knew he had houses in his name as well as theirs, and all during that time we'd lived in a rented flat that I'd paid for.

I started getting more involved with my new boyfriend and his life. He was like the dark side of the moon. I was fascinated by him and his mysterious life — it was one I'd never experienced, had always only observed.

Of course, I never told him what I did. I'd always leave his flat early in the morning, so he wouldn't get suspicious. As far as he knew I was working nine to five, temping in offices in the city. He seemed to sleep most of the day and would call me up at night.

I loved spending time with him, even though he could be really horrible. He would always deliver cutting remarks to me, and I'd always make cutting remarks back. I remember one night, when we'd been out to a few clubs and we'd been drinking quite heavily, I kept teasing him, saying that I wanted to have a different guy for every day of the week. When we were leaving the last club he kept saying he was going to kill me, and his eyes were glazed. He looked quite funny in the way he was saying it, and with the expression on his face, I never thought he meant it.

I'd always wanted to go to a dance party and Jordan took me to my first at Winterdaze. It was a gay dance party at the docks and I was looking forward to seeing how it would be. He said that he knew someone there who could score some Ecstasy. As I walked in, my eyes opened wide to see guys dressed in G-strings and costumes. I'd never had much to do with the gay community but I'd always thought that they were funny and witty. I felt quite shy amongst them, dressed so conservatively. Jordan was dressed casually in jeans and a sleeveless top. He went off to find his transsexual friend, who'd just finished dancing on stage, to see if he could score any Ecstasy.

I was quite happy being straight because it was all so new and exciting. After a few drinks Jordan came back, but he hadn't been able to score. Then later on he spotted one of his old schoolfriends, who was dealing acid. I knew that acid made you hallucinate and wasn't the same as speed or Ecstasy, but he didn't have anything else, so acid it was.

We took half each and at first I thought it was just paper because nothing happened until I was coming back from the toilets outside. I sure noticed the difference. I was walking through all the dancing bodies and I felt that I couldn't get out. I panicked, but found my way to the edge of the dance floor where I found Jordan. He said his trip had taken effect and he felt different, but he looked the same and he was talking the same. He didn't seem frightened the way I was. I tried to get into the dancing but every sensation was over-exaggerated and I kept hallucinating.

At the end of the night my mind was still wildly out of control, and I tried desperately to relax. I was glad I only had taken half a trip instead of a full one; then I would have been really fucked. I went home hoping my mind would return to normal. Jordan was still into his trip too, so we caught a cab back to his place. Lying in bed with him I kept thinking he was turning into a wolf. He was like a half-wolf, half-man, and I went to sleep hugging something hairy.

When I woke up from the acid I felt like I'd been on a marathon. It had taken a lot out of me, had scared me shitless, and I needed a day in bed to recover. I'd hated taking acid. I hadn't really enjoyed the dance party the entire time after the acid had taken over and I'd lost control over what I thought. I vowed I would never do acid again.

Jordan wasn't really into hard drugs either, although he was a big dope-smoker and could never wait to roll a joint. One night when I was over, instead of a joint he had a pipe, which he'd had in storage for a while at his friend's. The first time I pulled a pipe I coughed non-stop for fifteen minutes. I felt as if I was choking and when I stood up to get a glass of water I was really dizzy and nauseated.

I felt a lot more stoned on a pipe than I ever had on a joint, but after a week I got used to pulling pipes and started taking it like a professional — as Jordan said — without one cough. It was nice pulling a pipe anyway; I liked the sensation when I let go of the shotty and the smoke just hit me. It wasn't the stoned effect I liked, it was just the hit part.

I'd spend all night stoned with Jordan until six in the morning. I liked getting stoned because it was a big thrill for me to be on drugs, but Jordan always wanted the silent gaps to be filled in. So we'd always talk and I began to hate it. Usually when I wasn't talking he would be trying to fuck me. The sex had always been good but as our relationship passed the two-month mark, it started to go downhill. He was always just into fucking and licking my cunt. He never liked kissing and he rarely kissed my breasts. It was as if he thought I was just a hole and that was it.

The strangest thing about the situation was, I actually thought I loved him. When we had arguments, which was usually on the phone, he'd get crazy and tell me to fuck off. But I always wanted him no matter how mean he was to me. There was something about him that drew me to him. Everyone always said we looked good together, and we were well suited. I was not looking for a serious relationship and he knew that, but he'd always get very jealous if he saw another guy talking to me. In a way I liked that; I thought it was flattering.

I'd heard from his other friends, and he'd told me himself, that he used to beat up his ex-girlfriend quite badly. She was a lot younger than him at the time, still at school, and he was about nineteen. I knew he'd taken her from her parents' home because her stepdad used to beat her up, and then when he'd been with her for a while he started on her himself.

I never thought he'd do that to me. In fact I never thought anyone would hurt me. Although I was scared of men sometimes, I'd never been beaten. In all the years I'd worked, I'd come close to a few guys punching me in the head but I'd always got out of it.

Jordan moved from his flat in South Yarra into his dad's house in Tullamarine because he couldn't afford the rent any more. It was one of those houses that had two bedrooms, an open-plan kitchen and lounge. His dad was hardly ever there because he was mostly at his girlfriend's, so Jordan had the place to himself. He'd pick me up in his car, which was always breaking down, or I'd catch a taxi.

Things at Ted's had got really slow. Ted was still trying to give me money because he felt sorry for me — I was even beginning to feel sorry for myself. Maybe my outlook on life wasn't all that good. I always had enough for essentials, like rent and going out, but I'd be lucky if I earned three hundred a week — pretty depressing really: after all I *was* a prostitute.

Then a confession from Jordan turned my life around, and gave me a new outlook on my finances. It was one particular night when we'd only been drinking, since he hadn't been able to score any dope — he'd considered cutting his skin and getting stoned on Vegemite, but the thought of doing that made me feel sick. I'm not sure why he told me what he did: maybe he was sick of me and didn't care. We were just in the beginnings of having sex; he was naked and I had my hand on his cock getting him hard when he said that he'd been working as a prostitute.

It wasn't exactly a great shock. I knew that he'd driven transsexuals to escort bookings because he'd told me, but I didn't know he was a male prostitute. How ironic that out of everyone I could have met at a club, I'd met Jordan the prostitute. He went on to tell me how he'd lied to his girlfriend, the one he'd been living with for two years, and done bookings behind her back. And there was more. He was bi-sexual and he'd been doing gay bookings as well as women. He'd been sleeping with guys since he was young. He was a regular at the popular gay haunts and saunas, and he'd been seeing a transsexual on the nights I wasn't there in South Yarra.

I was fascinated by the fact he liked transsexuals. I wanted to know what it was like to have sex with a guy with tits and a cock. From what he said, it was pretty good. He told me that transsexuals worked on the streets mainly because they were always saving for their operation to make them into total women. He preferred sleeping with transsexuals to sleeping with men, but both turned him on.

The Prostitution Trap

I suppose at this stage I should have told him I was a prostitute as well. But it would have been too spooky, and too easy to confess to that, so I kept on lying, just as I'd done before.

When I woke up the next morning, I told him that I was sick of my nine-to-five job, and I wanted to work as a prostitute with him. He was shocked and half-joking he said it was something I'd have to think about, so I went home and, being smart, called him the next day to say I still wanted to work with him. Why not? I thought anything would have to be better than Ted's and his sympathy handouts.

From what Jordan had told me, working in the escort business was actually quite lucrative. He'd been working for an escort agency — the one he said he'd been driving for — and they got him bookings here and there, but he said there wasn't much demand for male hookers. He knew all about working privately. He knew where to advertise, how to advertise and how to talk to the clients on the phone. Working privately seemed like a great idea.

I told him the following day I definitely wanted to work with him and he agreed, although he was very surprised. He tried to talk me out of it, but then he just gave in with, 'If that's what you want'.

I paid for our first ad together in the Truth paper. It read 'Brooke, beautiful English Model' and underneath was 'Nick the Italian Stallion'. We used only a pager number because that's all we had. His dad was living at home on and off so we couldn't use a home number.

We didn't get any bookings the night the ad first went in, but then Jordan made some more confessions. He told me how he'd got his best friend, a Greek guy, to do bookings with him, but he hadn't been able to handle it. Not only that, but he'd been sleeping with him as well. There seemed no end to the people he'd been sleeping with — and to think he got jealous when guys tried to speak to me!

I hadn't used condoms since the first time I slept with him and often I was too stoned and enjoying it too much to stop or worry about condoms.

The next day the inquiries came through on his pager and seven out of ten were interested in me. Jordan would get on the phone and tell them my details. I was too scared to talk to them myself, so he'd arrange the booking. He drove me there and waited outside as security. I went into my first booking pretty frightened. I'd done escorts before, but never on such a personal level; it was always through a brothel and everything had been pre-arranged. Now it was up to me to take responsibility for the booking.

It was actually more exciting going out for a booking: I never knew what to expect. And unlike brothels, I never had to sit in the same place all night. There was at least some variety in people's homes. It was exciting going from house to house and I found the clients more interesting in their own environment; there was so much more to see than just a naked body, and of course, there was more money in it. Jordan had been advertising ourselves at a discount price, so we'd get more bookings than the rest of the ads. We were charging one hundred and twenty for an hour, and eighty dollars for half an hour. That was more than I ever got for selling my body and I didn't have to give any of the money to anyone. Or so I thought.

Chapter 9

Mad

I didn't discover it till it was too late, but Jordan was actually mad. He had always had that crazy distant look in his eyes, and he always said his mind never stopped, as though there were a million voices in there. But I thought he looked too cute, and he was too good in bed and funny, to be mad. Besides, I was having more fun than before, so it didn't matter. The problem was, the object of my desire kept getting worse and worse. While we hung around for the calls from the clients to come through, we spent all our time together. In the beginning it was fine. We'd get up after being stoned all night and doing bookings, and having sex in between, and eat out in a restaurant. I hadn't been home for ages, because Jordan hated it when I was with my friends. He wanted me around all the time. Besides I liked him by my side so I could hug him at night. I never felt lonely when he was there.

We hung out in gay clubs during the week and at weekends. I liked the crowd, who were always non-sleazy and good to be around. Jordan and I would drink away the money that we earned, and stay until early in the morning. Quite a few of our arguments started when I was drunk. It would begin over nothing and graduate into Jordan going into a sulky mood until we got back to his place, when he'd lose it and start smashing his fists into walls. I'd try to calm him down or just threaten to leave, and he'd stop. Until the next time.

Since Jordan didn't like me being with my friends, we hung out with his friends instead. And that was when the big surprise came. One of his friends recognised me from a brothel.

For the whole night Jordan said nothing until we were really stoned. I'd noticed that he wasn't his usual self, but I thought it must have been something I had said a week before: Jordan had a way of storing all his grudges over a period of time, then just exploding. But when he told me what he'd found out, he thought it was pretty cool, that I'd lied to him about not having worked as a prostitute before. He was badly stung, though, that someone was more shifty than he was. I had never thought of myself as shifty, just a better liar. But Jordan now thought that I was shifty. He wanted to know details of how long I'd worked. I confessed almost everything — only because I was stoned — and I told him the whole thing, right down to cheating behind my husband's back and getting residency through him, then leaving him.

Jordan sat there listening in silence to everything I had to say. His opinion of me changed greatly now that I had all these stories to show how shifty I was. He gave me little tell-tale signs of how completely untrustworthy I was, by never letting me out of his sight, in case I was fucking someone and he didn't see the money. He didn't have to tell me this — it was something I just worked out, but chose to ignore.

The more time I spent with him, the more I felt the need to get away from him, but what was I to do? Prostitution was all I'd known for years and it drew me to him along with the drugs that I'd taken. And despite it all, part of me loved him and couldn't let go.

Once he'd found out I'd been lying, he started to draw me more and more into his own world and his own way of thinking. It must have been because he could now relate to me better because he knew I was more like him. He saw it as the way God meant it to be. He went over how we'd both lied to our partners and worked behind their backs, and then ended up meeting each other in a club full of people. It had to be fate he said. I thought it was more like bad karma.

If I was ever meant to learn anything from what happened with Jordan, it was just to be careful. There's a million people out there and you just don't know what's going through their minds or what they are capable of doing.

In a matter of a month I'd become the very thing I

hated about most working girls. Without even realising it I'd been sucked in by a pimp. All the money we earned together — and most of it was mine — he persuaded me to pool, so we could start saving for a business together. Like most good con-artists, he made it sound very casual, like it didn't matter. I never got to see the money I earned, since it all went into his pocket.

I told myself I stayed with him because I loved him. Without him I'd never have had the chance to experience the things I now had. There was the sex, which had always been good, the dance parties and the dope, which was always easily available. And I didn't feel alone any more; Jordan always made me feel loved and wanted. To him I was beautiful and important.

Things got a bit quiet from our ad, so Jordan introduced me to a friend of his who owned a gay agency that he'd worked for before.

Ashley, who owned Boy Toys, was a sharp-witted, good-looking gay in his late thirties. He'd had a motorbike accident and lost one of his legs, so he had to hop around on crutches in his trendy third-floor apartment. There were cute-looking gay guys everywhere. They hung around while Ashley interviewed me. One was a make-up artist from Paris, who wanted to know whether I'd had a nose job. I took that as a compliment! I started doing lots more bookings after that. With two or three bookings a week from Ashley's, plus our own bookings, we started earning more money.

When Jordan advertised that we specialised in doubles and fantasies, our inquiries doubled. We had one inquiry from a gay man who was staying at a city hotel. He wanted us to make love in front of him and then for Jordan to suck him off. Before we went into the booking I quickly went to the reception toilet and saw that my period had come on. I was so relieved, because I was late, and because I had thought I was pregnant. The worst part was Jordan was furious because we didn't have time to go to a chemist to get a sponge.

Our client, Tom, was an American and he was overwhelmed with Jordan's huge cock and good looks. He wanted us to stay for a few hours and I thought grimly about my bleeding pussy, which would be obvious all over the white sheets.

Joints were rolled and passed around, and Tom offered us a bottle of amyl nitrate to sniff while we were having sex. Jordan had a bottle at home, which was yet another drug he'd introduced me to. The effect was an instant head rush that really got you into whatever you were doing at the time. I'd heard it could kill your brain cells quicker than anything else, so I tried to limit the temptation to sniff the stuff.

Tom was walking around in a T-shirt with his cock dangling out. He looked about fifty and was overweight. He had a mass of wild grey hair and stoned dark eyes that were looking at us under his glasses. Jordan and I were lying on the bed, Jordan's head between my legs and me lying back with a joint between my lips. I could feel blood dripping out of my cunt and I felt sorry for Jordan who would have been doing a good impersonation of Dracula. Tom then wanted to see Jordan fuck me and he kept encouraging him, while at the same time taking huge sniffs of amyl nitrate. Then I saw Jordan suck his cock while I lay on the bed and watched. It was the first time I'd seen two guys together in real life, and I thought it looked very sexy. Both their cocks went really hard and while Jordan's cock was that hard Tom wanted him to fuck me with it. He thought I was sweet and cute and well worth the money. And he had plenty of it.

When he paid us seven hundred dollars at the end of the night for staying for five hours, Jordan thought he'd hit the big time. I was too stoned and too tired, but Jordan would have been the happiest I'd ever seen him, and he wanted me to cook him scrambled eggs when we got home. And I did, before I went to sleep.

We started doing more double bookings after that; all we had to do was have sex in front of the clients, and that was it. Either one of us would suck them off, depending whether they were gay or straight. Jordan always had stage fright and his cock would never go that hard, but we both could act well, so it was easily covered up and between us we made quite a good sex show.

Jordan had a number of regular gay clients and a few were interested in seeing me, since he'd told them all about me. His clients were nice and they always had a joint and a witty comment. Jordan, on the other hand was a typical pimp, and they all made funny comments, warning me about him when he went out of the room. They knew him only too well.

My sleeping with men made him jealous, but he liked the money I made. He always contradicted himself. On a Saturday night after a few bongs, he'd go over all the things I'd done wrong for the week, but they were so minor they were hardly worth mentioning, like the time I ran water for the kettle while he was taking a shower, or if I'd mentioned that one client was good in bed.

I started to realise how dangerous he actually was when we were out one night at a club. We'd been drinking quite heavily, and he bumped into one of his old working friends from an agency where he used to work. His name was Rob and he was rather cute. I'd been asking Jordan recently for a threesome and this seemed like the ideal opportunity. We chatted for a while then went back to Rob's place, where he was living with a client of his. We all sat down on the bed with a bottle of vodka and drank. I watched as they started kissing and undressing each other. Rob reached over to kiss me and Jordan pulled my blouse undone and cupped my breasts. They started sucking on my nipples and Rob put his hand inside my pants to rub my pussy. I was so turned on, but I'd drunk too much. I sucked on one's cock while the other fucked me from behind.

I watched as Rob slipped his cock inside Jordan, who was now kneeling on the bed. He slid his cock in and out and I looked at Jordan's face as he was getting fucked. He looked different in that position. But I'd drunk way too much, and I threw up on the bed, and fell unconscious. I heard Rob just giggling and reaching over to change the sheets, but Jordan was furious. He pulled me off to the bathroom and asked me what was wrong. I remember just sitting in the shower, letting the water spill all over me as I listened to Jordan nag on. When we were all back in bed I fell asleep, and they carried on fucking. In the morning I told Jordan that he didn't care about me, and he reached over to put his hands around my neck as if to strangle me. If Rob hadn't been there he would have carried on with the job.

After that I was always more wary of Jordan and I even thought about leaving him and going back home. I wasn't happy and he was so unpredictable that I was beginning to become very frightened of him. But there was always tomorrow, and maybe he would calm down. Anyway I was now used to having so many bongs that I was less cautious about what was happening around me. If I'd been straight I'd have been out of there right away.

So much for tomorrow. I had started to get bruises on my arms from his outbursts and he'd begun threatening me. He had told me of a time in Sydney when he was robbing a gay guy in the toilets with a friend. Before they did it, Jordan was sniffing amyl nitrate and he beat the guy to death, or so he said. I thought at the time he was joking, but now I wasn't so sure.

I started to dread going to the bookings from Ashley's. He advertised under a gay ad and most of the clients were bi-sexuals. But they weren't like the cute, gorgeous guys that we saw in clubs; they were smelly, disgusting things. They were usually really weird, and I didn't know where the hell he got them from.

The worst escort booking I ever did was from an ad I had with Jordan. I'd been waiting outside the client's flat in the car when Jordan came out and said the client wanted a double. He had been very quiet on the way to the booking, and I wondered just how bad this was going to be. When we got back inside I found that the whole place just stank and amongst the rotting furniture and the dirty dishes stood this naked guy who was about sixty. He was grossly overweight and sweating profusely, and he didn't seem to be all there. He wanted to watch Jordan and me have sex on the bed, and he wanted to touch me too. I felt sick. If I'd been Jordan I wouldn't have accepted this booking, but instead he made it easier on himself by pulling me into it. It was like being in hell for half an hour. How could Jordan do something like that to me?

After that my opinion of him went right down. Now I actually disliked him. I saw him for what he was, a pimp boyfriend who would threaten me if I didn't stay with him. He knew I was scared and he knew he had me.

It was coming to the end of 1993 and I decided that I would have to set a deadline for leaving Jordan — before the New Year. I'd got myself into this situation and I could get myself out. I just hoped I'd do it in time. But the strangest thing was that after everything he'd done to me, and after knowing about every other sick thing he'd done, my heart still felt for him. At times, I even still loved him.

I must have been addicted to the abuse. He liked playing with my mind and making me cry, and then he'd give me a bong and hug me and be all nice again. It was like submissive sex, but worse, because I never knew where it would begin or end.

Jordan and I had saved close to five thousand dollars under his couch. He said we could split it any time we wanted but he never left me alone; he was afraid that I'd steal it. It was actually hardly anything, but to him it was a big deal. For years he had very little and he thought we were just at the beginning of the money. He wanted to reach about sixty thousand dollars, and he came up with the idea of getting a flat together and working from there. He said he wanted to start getting hormone injections, so he could have breasts and work as a transsexual. I thought it was just another one of his mind games, but he was really quite serious. He went as far as buying a wig and dressing up at home.

Watching him tottering around in high heels and a blond wig, with make-up on his face, was too much. At first I thought it was funny but he kept on saying how serious he was about being a transsexual; he really didn't like being a man — he wanted to be a woman. It was all too sudden. I tried to be understanding but I wasn't sure whether he would go through with the hormone treatment.

I tried to put all this aside and not worry about it; I wanted to talk mindless chit-chat all the time like Jordan, so I didn't have to think about anything. I was turning into a mess. I started to become paranoid from all the dope I was smoking, I got jumpy and nervous in bookings, and I felt like a zombie.

Jordan liked taking valium because it relaxed him, and he would think nothing of taking two or three a night to sleep better. I took them with him and it made me feel better too. It blocks all feeling out of your body and when you wake up in the morning you feel numb and senseless, as if you aren't really alive.

Christmas was only a day away, and Jordan scored some acid. He said he hated Christmas and wanted to be out of it. There wasn't much else to do, so we took acid with a cousin of his who had been staying over and smoking dope. His cousin had hung out with skinheads for years and he'd done a stack of drugs, but his favourite was acid.

The Prostitution Trap

I took only a quarter because that was all I needed, but Jordan and his cousin took a full one each. We caught a cab to a pub in the city owned by one of Jordan's friends. The trip started coming on in the cab. My heart-beat started up and I felt more conscious and awake. We got out of the cab and walked into the pub. I'd met Tony, the friend who owned the pub, a few times before. He was a self-made millionaire and sleazy and cruel with it. He'd liked me since he first saw me, and wanted to fuck me. Jordan was like Tony's protege; he'd sit and talk with Jordan and tell him how to rip people off. He knew that Jordan worked and he knew that I worked as well.

It was about twelve o'clock and closing time, and the place was full of off-duty police. All the cops were drunk and enjoying the free booze. I knew Tony was involved in criminal activities and it was probably pay-off time. When the acid hit me I was by the pool table and everything that Jordan and Tony talked about seemed hilarious, and I couldn't stop laughing. My stomach ached from laughing so much, and I thought I was having a great time. Tony had a trip and so did Manuel, Jordan's best friend. I suddenly became nervous when I noticed I was the only girl there. We had planned to go on and party at a few clubs, but I didn't really have it together enough to call a cab, and I drifted off to the toilet feeling giddy. I sat in there for about five minutes waiting for my mind to calm down.

When I walked out, Jordan and Tony were at the pinball machine with a few of the cops. Jordan's cousin came over to me saying that one of the cops hadn't had sex in ages because his wife was pregnant. I was nervous and I could hardly breathe. Some more guys joined me and I felt hemmed in. For one second I imagined that it was a scene from a bad movie, with me about to be raped. They were all cops. Everything would have been over in an hour, and it would have all been covered up. I thought maybe Jordan had set me up with all these cops; I wouldn't put anything past him. I ran to the door and called Tony over to unlock it. He did, smirking. Relief spread through me, as the fresh air engulfed me. I felt safe now. Maybe I'd saved myself from one more nightmare.

After that, the night took a dive and, although I tried to have a good time, I kept thinking about the panic I'd felt at the pub. I was nervous and I wanted to go home. Jordan said I was up and down all the time, and I was. Maybe I was the one who was mad after all.

At around six in the morning, we all got in a cab and went home. Jordan and his cousin were still tripping and they wanted to take another once we were inside. Jordan wanted to spend the whole of Christmas day tripping off his head. He and his cousin kept sniffing amyl nitrate and I was coming down with a bang. I felt very emotional, scared and all over the place. Jordan kept on saying there were things he wanted to talk to me about, and he wanted to be off his face while he was doing it.

It was another scene from hell. The lounge was smashed up from a row we'd had before, and Jordan had thrown everything everywhere. A cat he had bought me as a present looked all frightened and scared. I tried to look after it while I was there, but his cousin had got hold of it when we'd been out and had been giving it amyl nitrate so it looked all fucked up.

Although I hadn't been back in ages I caught a cab

home, to escape the nightmare, but I couldn't get away from it. I was coming down and I couldn't sleep, and I spent the entire day worrying, trying to call Jordan. I knew he had a stack of acid at his place, and I thought maybe he would try and kill himself. Each time he picked up the phone he said how he understood women now. And he'd really thought about it.

I knew from what he was saying that he was having a hard time. He would have been tired and hungry, and the acid would have taken full effect. He said he felt as if he was in a glass bottle and he couldn't get out, and he kept on asking me how to do it. I tried to calm him down but the more I tried the worse he got. He said he was going to take the rest of the acid and it was because of me. I felt so responsible for what I'd done to this person. Even if he was mad, he hadn't been this bad when I first met him.

I talked him out of it and called the drug information line. Jordan wanted me to bring him over some dope but I was too scared; I thought dope would just increase the effects of the tripping. The drug line said that he'd need to drink and eat to bring him down, but I wasn't completely convinced that he wanted to come down.

I sent him pizza and orange juice and prayed that would help him. He kept calling me every half-hour to let me know how he felt. That night he came around and he seemed okay. He called one last time to say that he loved me, and because I'd sent him all those pizzas, it showed that I cared.

I was so emotionally stressed out with the events of the past day that I even called my mum in England; she was having dinner with my brother. She seemed surprised to hear from me and was really distant. I told her how much I loved her, and she snorted with laughter, no doubt because I hadn't written or phoned in ages. I just wanted her to say that she loved me back. I'd never been emotional with her, but I just wanted to hear it from her. I wanted to hear her say that she loved me because I was her daughter. Afterwards, I felt as if I had nobody that I could turn to, that I was pretty much alone in the world. In a way, her distance pushed me closer to Jordan, who said he loved me.

I went to sleep at the end of this very stressful day and woke up feeling better. I vowed I would never take acid again. I called Jordan to see how he was, and he was full of apologies for the day before. He said he was now over acid and he didn't do it anymore. I believed him. I just wanted to be in his arms again. I needed him and I needed someone to love me. Being with Jordan was easy. Even though he beat me up, threatened me and abused me, it was better than being unloved and alone.

The problem was he knew too much about me. He knew where to hit me emotionally, where it would hurt. He knew about my brother and my past; he knew practically everything about me. His nickname for me was Big Eyes. I had told him about how I used to sit on the window-ledge when I was young, looking at the cars going past, desperately wishing one of them would take me out of my life, to some place else. He thought that name suited me; I thought it sounded really dorky. It made me feel really small, yet he still teased me with it. Jordan sometimes reminded me of my brother, and from certain angles he even looked like him, especially when I was stoned.

The Prostitution Trap

I think all that acid had had an effect on Jordan's mind. We didn't do any bookings for a few days and stayed at home smoking. I was still very jumpy around him and every time he made me a drink I would panic, thinking he'd spiked it with the acid he had left. I couldn't trust him at all. He would frighten me and make me laugh at the same time. He would go into graphic detail about what he would do to me if I tried to leave him. First he'd put me in a locked room, and then force feed me acid and put a snake in there, and I'd be tied up to a chair, so I couldn't move and he'd watch from a window to see what I would do as the snake curled around me. He knew I was terrified of snakes.

He tormented me about being mad and how I should be locked up in a mental hospital. There seemed no end to the things he wanted to do to me. And on top of all that he was religious. He said he believed in God and everything that was written in the Bible, particularly everything that was written about women. He thought women were meant to serve men and that I was the worst kind of woman. I was a cheat and a whore, and I deserved to pay for my sins. When he started preaching verses from the Bible I thought he'd really lost it. I believed in God but I didn't believe everything in the Bible, and I hated people preaching to me.

And then came New Year and the chain of events I had probably been waiting for. On New Year's Eve there was another dance party on, Jordan had two tabs of acid left and he said, what was the harm in taking a bit more? I sort of agreed; we had to spend New Year doing something, and there certainly was no better way than being at a dance party on drugs.

So we took acid again and went to the dance party. It was great. I felt more relaxed, except for a few tense moments when I thought there was a snake next to me. We wandered around and saw Ashley who was handing out cards for his agency. He started telling me I should be a model, and that I was too good to be a prostitute. He said he could help me if I wanted.

The acid didn't have a bad effect on me this time and I got into dancing with Jordan, and we kept sniffing more amyl nitrate. Time seemed to go too quickly and it was soon time to welcome 1994. So much for my resolution of leaving him by the New Year .

Jordan's dad had no control over him and even though he'd told him to get the carpet in the lounge dry-cleaned, Jordan hadn't bothered. We slept for most of the next few days and then I called someone to come around and clean the carpet. I was asleep in bed when he came the next day, and I quickly got up and put on jeans and T-shirt to answer the door. He was a nice guy who did a good job. I made him a drink and sat talking with him for a while, just to be polite. Jordan was in bed listening to the whole thing. When I went in with a glass of water, he just gave me a threatening look. Gut instinct told me to get out: Jordan was going to lose his temper really badly this time. I nearly left; I nearly told the dry cleaning man that something was wrong, that I was in danger. But I ignored my instincts and stayed. I would have looked too much like a fool. I would leave Jordan properly, not like a fugitive.

Jordan started on me as soon as the cleaner left, and I knew that my chance had gone. Whatever was going to happen now, I'd have to see it through, although I knew the danger signs. He told me to go and get the bong and he went to get the dope. There was still heaps left, and he wanted me to start smoking it. It was in the afternoon and I didn't particularly want to get stoned right now, but he handed me the bong and ordered me to have it. I didn't really have a choice.

After about three bongs I got frightened and said I didn't want any more. He got angry and said if I didn't keep going he'd hold the bottle of amyl nitrate under my nose until I did. As soon as he mentioned amyl, I agreed to have as many bongs as he wanted. He said he was going to get me completely wasted, and then he was going to get a bottle of champagne out of the fridge and make me drink that too. Or else he would smash it over my head.

I was so scared, but at the same time I felt sorry for myself. With the effects of so many bongs I felt a complete sense of loneliness, that there wasn't one person who cared for me. Jordan thought I was just after sympathy and he hated it when girls cried. He lunged at me and put his hands around my neck and I began to choke for air. When he was dangerously close to finishing me off, he suddenly let go. I gasped to fill my lungs, and my throat hurt. He then threw me onto the ground and packed me another pipe. He wanted me really out of it. Thank God there was no acid left.

While his head was turned, packing the pipe, I crept towards the door. I'd made it to the lounge before he was behind me, trying to grab me. As I ran out the door I screamed, hoping at least one of the neighbours would come to my rescue, but he was right behind me, and he dragged me back inside with his hand over my mouth. Throwing me against the wall, he head-butted me, pulled me back into the bedroom and threw me back onto the floor. Then he grabbed hold of my hair and slapped my face really hard.

He had a crazy look in his eyes, and I knew now that it was life or death. I'd had plenty of warning; now I was facing the reality that he was very dangerous. He kept saying that I could easily go missing and that no-one would know, but that even death wasn't good enough for me. He wanted to keep me alive so he could torture me. On and on his sick mind went about what he was going to do. And I knew if I didn't do some fast talking he was really going to carry it out this time.

Now that my life was at risk I knew more than ever that I didn't want to die. I'd had so many pipes I should have been out of it, but I was clear in my mind that I had to calm Jordan down somehow, that I could get out of this. I was a survivor, and now I had the instincts of an animal, and a courage that came from deep within. The times I'd thought that I would be better off dead were gone; I wanted to be alive more then anything and I would not give in.

Somehow I managed to talk him out of the idea of being with me. I said it would be better for him if we split up, that we weren't suited and he could go his way, and I'd go mine, and we'd never see each other again. I agreed with everything he said: I was no good and I had a lot to learn. He agreed, and he seemed to come around to my way of thinking. First he said he'd call me a taxi to take me home, and I thought that was it, that I was safe. But then he offered to give me a lift home. I didn't want to disagree — my mistake — and I got in the car thinking everything was fine.

Once I was in, he reached over and pushed down the lock so I couldn't get out. When he turned around to me he still had that crazy look in his eyes. Now I was in his car, he said, he was going to take me where I belonged — the mental hospital, where Big Eyes was going to spend the rest of her life looking out of barred windows.

By this stage I felt nothing but hate for him; I wasn't even scared any more. I didn't think a mental hospital would take me in, even if he knew someone there. But I did know that he had a lot of strange clients.

Even though I was scared, I felt stronger than him. I hated him so much, there was no way he was taking me anywhere.

On the outskirts of town we had to stop at a red light and I thought this might have been my last chance. As we stopped he had a grip on my arm but I pulled away from him, opened the door and jumped out. There was a petrol station just ahead and I ran towards it. Jordan turned his car around and sped off.

Somehow I managed to explain that a crazy boyfriend had tried to kill me. I was really traumatised and just wanted to hide because I was terrified that he would come back for me.

I sat and wondered if I'd ever feel safe again. But at least the events of the past few days had broken the emotional ties that had bound me to Jordan.

Chapter 10

Sydney again

Being nearly killed brought home to me how much I really liked living. For a long time I think I'd been slowly trying to kill myself. Now I'd been through hell, life had started to look pretty good. I still felt I was partly in shock, and I was jumpy and scared that Jordan would find me again any minute.

Apparently he'd told one of my friends that I'd freaked out and tried to commit suicide. I told them what had really happened, and after a few days at a hotel I went home.

I felt scared about being in Melbourne, and I hated the idea that Jordan was around. I decided that maybe it would be better if I went to Sydney for a while. I needed a break from Melbourne, I reasoned, and it would be as if I was leaving the past behind.

The whole episode had a huge effect on me, and it didn't really make sense to go to a state where I knew no one, but that's what I did.

I spoke to Jordan on the phone before I left Melbourne. He'd been calling non-stop. He said that he was sorry for what he'd done and he wanted us to be friends. He said he hadn't been taking me anywhere that day; he had been just trying to scare me and that was all. I nearly believed him. I began to think that maybe I'd over-reacted and I needed to calm down. That gave me all the more reason to go to Sydney. I really needed to get away from things: I needed time to myself.

It was January and Sydney was hot. I stayed at one of the hotels in Kings Cross. I spent the first few days pondering whether I'd done the right thing. I even thought about going back to Jordan but managed to stop myself in time. I was glad of the distance between us.

I found a place to live in Darlinghurst at two hundred dollars a week, and when my furniture came from Melbourne I settled into my new apartment. It was nice and peaceful living by myself and having no shadows following me around. I was free to do what I wanted and to go where I pleased. I'd taken the twenty thousand dollars I had from my security deposit box for emergencies. Sydney was very expensive, mind you, and it was easy to spend thousands of dollars very quickly. In a matter of days, I'd splashed out four thousand, just on bond money, new furniture and living expenses.

I had every intention of working privately and as soon as I had everything ready I put an ad in The Naughty Sydney magazine. The response was good. I'd used my home number, and I got non-stop calls day and night. I hadn't spoken to clients on the phone before, and at first I think I was too nice. I thought everyone was genuine, but most were just wankers pulling their cocks off to the sound of my voice. I had a few clients around, but some were pretty weird, and they made me nervous. My apartment was tucked away in a quiet area, and one client summed it up one night when he said, 'What if I had a gun or a knife? What would you do then?'

He was right. I didn't think Sydney was the right place to work privately, which was a shame really because that is what I'd intended to do. But Sydney was too much of a big city. There would be more risks here, and too many weirdos.

So I did what I normally did: I got a job at another brothel. It was at the Black Cat this time and it catered for massage and pully-pully, as the girls called it, as well as full service. The massage girls said they weren't as fucked up as the girls who worked as prostitutes, because they didn't have sex with the clients; they just massaged them naked and then pulled them off by hand. And they were right. It was actually quite a nice, relaxing atmosphere. They were always playing Enya and other nice quiet music in the background. There was no pressure and the girls always took little snoozes when they were tired. The clients were mainly Asians and middle-aged men and no-one gave me a hard time.

I met one Asian client I will be eternally grateful to —

he taught me how to masturbate until I could come. This was something I could never do before. I could make myself come with a vibrator but they always made a noise. He showed me how to play with my clit, to rub it and to think of enough of my fantasies to make myself come. I had always had to rely on men's tongues, but now I felt very independent with my new skill. I was able to keep myself satisfied, which was just as well because there were so many gay guys in Sydney, and so much competition from other girls.

I'd joined a trendy gym in the hope of getting healthy. I got a personal trainer just to get fit, but when I started looking at how beautiful everyone else was, I became insecure and wanted a body just like theirs. Although I trained for a long time at that gym and got fit, I still had alopecia and I still didn't look that much better.

I hadn't made any friends and I was dreadfully unhappy. I met groups of people in clubs who were nice and wanted to be friends but I didn't feel as if I fitted in. Everyone seemed so together and the girls all looked the part, and I felt such a dag. I wasn't as smart as they were, and I didn't look as good, and I didn't act cool on drugs, which is something they all did. So many girls in Sydney were bi-sexual and girlfriends were always kissing-friends from what I saw. At one club I'd just met a guy and he introduced me to a girl who said 'Hi, I'm Lori'. She then said to me, 'Are you bi?' When I said yes, she started kissing me. She had lipstick on and I could taste it as I kissed her, and she had huge breasts that I softly touched. It felt unusual kissing a girl. I didn't find it sexual at all, just awkward. She was too small, and I had to crouch down to kiss her.

Sydney again

I started doing kickboxing as well as training at the gym, and it made me feel stronger and more in control. I was quite good at it and I had a strong kick. I always thought of Jordan when I was hitting the bag; it was good therapy. I still thought of him a lot, and I felt sorry for what I'd done to him. I thought maybe I had pushed him too far. Since I'd been working with him and he'd found out I'd lied about my past, the arguments had got worse and out of control and I had stuck around long after seeing the first danger signals. I blamed myself for what had happened. I still loved him in a crazy sort of way and I was still trying to get over him. I thought about the fun we'd had before he tried to kill me, and about the times when he used to sing to me and he sounded so beautiful. The last time I'd spoken to him he'd said that he wished me every happiness in the world. I wish he hadn't said it because it cut right through me.

I wasn't happy, but I still carried on. I didn't feel that I belonged in Sydney, but I wasn't about to go back to Melbourne either. Not yet, not even if I was spending more money than I was making (my savings had gone down drastically). Instead of having twenty thousand I now only had ten, and I'd only been in Sydney about four months. I was thinking about working privately again; it was easier than working all night for the same money that I could get from a few clients at home. I hadn't the motivation to do much nowadays; in fact the idea of actually doing anything made me go back to bed to think about it first.

Then came along James. I was working one night at the Black Cat and he booked me. He was from China, he told me after we'd had sex. He was skinny and he had part of his lung missing, and when he was fucking me in doggy position, he was pratically gasping for air. He lit a cigarette and offered one to me, and then asked me whether I wanted to work for him. It was quite common for other brothel owners to go in to an opposition brothel and poach the girls that would suit their own brothel the best, or they might send in one of their men to do it for them. James had a place in Burwood where he had Asian girls working for him, and he needed a Western girl. It was, of course, an illegal brothel, but he said he had protection, so it was safe. I could make five hundred a night and I only had to work from six until midnight. It seemed like a good deal; the Black Cat had been dead for ages and six hours work for five hundred dollars seemed a fair deal — if it was true and if it was safe.

The first night I walked in there I was pleasantly surprised by a huge house, nicely decorated, and with six dogs barking outside. James wasn't there, but a Chinese girl called Melissa was waiting for me. She took me into a room, one of four bedrooms, and asked me to show her what I had to wear. She was talking to me in a hushed voice and when she spoke it sounded as if she was saying something very important and secretive.

She said the clients were all Chinese, and I was to charge them ninety dollars, but I wasn't to say anything to the rest of the girls because they charged only eighty-five, and it might upset them. There weren't exactly that many girls there to say it to. Sitting in the kitchen watching Melissa cook were two other Asian girls, one Chinese, who couldn't speak much English, and the other one Korean, who spoke English well.

Melissa was tall and she had pretty features, large eyes and long shiny hair that I instantly felt jealous of. My hair was thin and long and it had no life as it had before. I was still good-looking at twenty-four but I looked unhealthy. James was right; I did make five hundred that night. I saw client after client. I thought it would be easy because Asian clients were normally quick and trouble-free, but I was a Westerner in a Chinese place, and I had a feeling some of the clients were racist and not very nice. They were different from the clients at brothels. They were more particular and they were rougher and more cutting. They pulled at my breasts and nipples until by the end of the night they were sore from being sucked at. I still hated clients kissing my breasts; I didn't care if they licked my cunt but I hated the sensation of their mouth on my nipples. To me that was about as personal as it could get.

The Chinese clients loved a massage first, and they'd plonk themselves on the bed so I could give them a back rub before turning them over to fuck them. Melissa told me to tell them that I was from Italy. I didn't think I looked Italian and neither did the clients, but it sounded more exotic than saying I was from England. The clients would be very disappointed if I didn't speak a few words in Italian, and the only ones I really knew sounded as if they came from a menu.

In the first few weeks I was non-stop busy. At the end of six hours I would have seen ten clients and I would be very tired. Melissa would cook us dinner and charge us ten dollars at the end of the night for it. She said she wanted this business for a year, then she said, 'Finish, because too much trouble from the girls'.

The Prostitution Trap

I liked most of the girls working there. Mimi was the Chinese girl, and she was the youngest. She'd worked for six months and saved fifty thousand dollars. For that she'd worked seven days a week for nearly six months, and she said sometimes she would see sixteen clients in a day and night. She'd mentioned something about starting some sort of business back home in China. Melissa had taken her in as part of the family and let her sleep at the house, so she'd be able to save money more quickly. It looked to me, however, as if she had overworked and her relationship with James and Melissa was a bit rocky.

Now she only did part service because she was bleeding all the time from a period that wouldn't stop. Her English was quite bad but when she spoke she sounded so cute. She was terribly naive, and I had a feeling that Melissa might have used Mimi to make a lot of quick money.

The rest of the girls were older, in their early twenties, and most were from Korea. James had found them in other brothels, and a few working as low-paid kitchen hands, because they were only here on student visas. They liked me and we got on well together. I spent a lot of time by myself reading in my room, and it was nice to work in a place where I could have so much space to myself. There were no drug-crazy girls walking around and speeding off their faces; it was quiet and peaceful. The only interruptions came from the clients.

I wasn't the only one who got the rough clients, who took great pleasure in pulling your body around the bed as if it was made of rubber — the Korean girls suffered it too. James and Melissa would say our job was easy because the clients all had small dicks, but their attitude towards us sucked.

I stayed working at James's place for a few months until most of the clients had seen me, and then I started getting less bookings. They advertised only in the Chinese newspaper, and they only had so many clients, so once you weren't new that was it. The next new girl came along for them all to try.

I decided to move from Darlinghurst to shared accommodation at Bondi Junction. I'd had enough of paying two hundred dollars a week and I was worried that I was spending too much time alone. When I wasn't working I rarely went out, unless it was to go to the gym. I'd become a gym junkie, but I still didn't have a life. The people I got to share with were a couple, she a manager of a hotel and he in advertising. As soon as she mentioned advertising my ears pricked up. I'd always been interested in advertising.

I moved in and at first I liked being around them. They tried to make me welcome but I felt I was intruding because they were a couple, something I hadn't thought of before. We didn't really have much to say after the initial pleasantries of moving in, and we didn't feel that comfortable in each other's company. I had a feeling they just suffered lodgers, because they needed the extra money to pay off the mortgage.

I quit working at James's and got a job working nights at the weekend at a brothel in the suburbs. I'd heard from the Black Cat that it was really busy and you could make a thousand dollars in two nights. So I gave Midnight Express a go. If it meant keeping awake until six in the morning, just two nights a week, it wouldn't be that bad. The prices were pretty low and when they told me I'd only get thirty-five dollars for half an hour I almost walked out. At that price what were the clients going to be like? I was about to walk out when I realised there weren't that many places in Sydney where you could make better money. I'd tried a few of the up-market places and I'd been back to Lilies, but I was no longer nineteen years old, and I didn't look as fresh and cute as I used to. The nights I did work I'd get no bookings, or just a few. It was really depressing.

So what if I'd ended up in a cheap suburban brothel four years later? I might as well make the most of it and face the reality of it all. Actually I didn't end up doing many half-hour bookings, but more twenty-minute bookings that I got twenty dollars for.

The girls were the worst I'd ever met. They were hardened workers who had been hard at it for years. They were so bitchy and mean, and the boss was some Turkish guy who hated me as soon as I opened my mouth. I ended up seeing about thirteen clients until I was so tired I could hardly stand. I caught the train home at six in the morning to Bondi, thinking maybe this wasn't such a good idea after all.

But where was I going to go? I needed the cash and what were a few harsh days out of seven? I could always suppress the bad memories — they could join the queue with the rest.

It was around this time that I found another patch of hair missing from my scalp. The stress from working at such a hell-hole was obviously showing. Maybe the time had come when I couldn't go on treating my body any-old-how.

Maybe the late nights were doing it to me. So after a month of working there, I quit and gave James a call. James and Melissa had had a break from working because a lot of girls had quit or gone on holiday around the same time I had left. But recently a few girls had been calling them for work, so they'd got another place in a different area.

Their new place wasn't as good as the huge house they'd rented before. Now they had just a small terraced place that was half the size. There weren't as many clients as before, and the first week was very slow. I was glad I wasn't working at Midnight Express any more; at least now I could go home at eleven o'clock at night instead of six in the morning. I had to work longer hours now because they'd just started their business again and they said it would take them a while to get it running.

After a few weeks, when the old clients realised Melissa and James were back in business, it got busy again, and some days we went back to earning four or five hundred. The clients were actually worse than before: we were in a rougher area and I had to take great care with the difficult ones who could turn aggressive towards me. I remember being in tears from a client who wanted to fuck me twice in half an hour, but I wouldn't let him. He got frantic to the point of hurting me physically and I burst out crying in the room from sheer frustation, something I'd never done before. I left the room crying as I pulled my clothes on and went to have a shower to try and recover.

Melissa came in and saw how upset I was. She sympathised and told me the client had gone and had apologised for making me cry. But his friend wanted to see me. Did I want to see him?

The Prostitution Trap

I knew that Melissa had worked in a brothel in Melbourne because the rest of the girls had told me. She was not really that understanding but at times she meant well — I think.

It was around four weeks into working, that Melissa and James started being hassled by the Vietnamese gangs. They didn't want to pay them any more protection money than they were already. I didn't fully understand what was going on but Mimi, who was on reception at the time, explained they wanted too much protection money. Melissa stood her ground and hired a security guard for a week to protect us from the Vietnamese gangs, but that didn't stop them. There were quarrels and fights until finally we got our warning.

I was upstairs in the bathroom combing my hair when I turned around and there was a gun in my face. The man wore a scarf around the lower half of his face, and at first I thought it was James mucking around with a toy gun, until he pointed it at my head and put a hand over my mouth. He told me if I kept quiet and did as he said I wouldn't get hurt. At first I couldn't fully comprehend the situation. He led me down the stairs with the gun pointed at me. I realised it must be one of the Vietnamese gangs. Everyone was downstairs kneeling on the floor, with their heads facing the floor. There were only two gang members and the other one was asking Melissa where the money was. She said that James had it and he'd be back soon. I knew she was lying because she kept most of the money hidden in one of the cupboards. But money was worth a lot to Melissa. Even if these men had guns, she wasn't about to tell them where it was. I admired her bravery but I thought she was foolish to risk our lives over money.

As it turned out they weren't after much. It was more of a warning than anything. I was half expecting them to shoot someone, but as soon as they had the money they left. We all sighed with relief when they sped off in their van.

Melissa called James to come straight away and we all sat around wondering what was going to happen next. I was frightened they'd come back, so I left, with a Korean girl who was living in my area. I remember we were standing together in McDonald's and for one brief moment I think I lost my mind. It might have been too many drugs, too many late nights and too much violence, but for an instant everything seemed hazy and I wondered whether it was okay to be insane, because that's how I felt. I'd always tried to talk myself out of insanity before but this time I couldn't be bothered. I just let my mind go until I came back to reality.

I decided I had to get out of Sydney. Nothing had gone right since I'd got here. I'd managed to spend almost all the money I'd saved — I only had about a thousand dollars left. But I had a car, which was the best thing I'd bought. It could take me from Sydney back to Melbourne, and I'd write off the last eight months as a bad mistake.

Before I left I was mooching around the library looking for books about dreams, and I came across a book called Superlearning. It explained how accelerated learning could open up parts of the brain that were previously untapped. If there was a way I could use more brain cells, it had to be good. I needed to change my life. I needed to do something. I left the book in Sydney but I remembered the name and made a mental note to get it in a Melbourne library.

Chapter 11

Brad

Coming into Melbourne was a relief. It was good to be back 'home' again. It was early December and I was looking forward to Christmas. I moved into a small flat in South Yarra, and put an ad in the Truth straight away. I needed the money after paying out the rest of what I had left for a bond.

The response was good, and the first night the advertisement came out, I made an easy four hundred dollars after seeing only three clients. Melbourne clients were more relaxed and easy to deal with; there were no surprises — they just paid their money and I did my job.

I felt a bit uncomfortable that I was living where I was

working, and sleeping with clients in the same bed that I slept in. I lost a lot of privacy and I thought about living somewhere else. I had a security flat so I felt safe, but I hated clients looking at my belongings, and worse still, some clients went through my wardrobe when I left them to get changed.

I spent Christmas and New Year alone in my flat. I was glad that I was back in Melbourne, but I was spending more time by myself. I didn't want to go out or do anything with friends. I wasted hours doing nothing, and most of the time just thinking of the things I wanted to do. I became very lazy and unmotivated. I thought about my future and what I wanted to do, but I hadn't anything mapped out, except maybe a few more years working. Then I'd do something else. I never thought much about getting a straight job; I would have been able to do only casual, unskilled work, and I had no career aspirations.

When I was young I'd always dreamt about being a beautiful model on the covers of magazines. Unfortunately I had a bad squint which was only corrected in my teenage years, so I grew up feeling ugly having being teased for too long. I never got to be the beautiful model I'd aspired to be.

Somehow I felt drawn back to the Meeting Place. I'd been driving around late at night in South Yarra, listening to the sound track of Natural Born Killers. I felt I was in a different world from everyone else, and the Meeting Place was the only place that was so bad that I felt drawn back to it, like a spider to its web.

My old haunt had been renovated and no longer did it look like the sleazy brothel that it once was. The first thing

I noticed was the old hostess, who had been there before. She was standing at reception dressed in black undies and suspenders, looking about ten years older. I was amazed to see that she was working, when she had always denied she would.

I walked inside the girls' room, which now looked more like a doctor's surgery. There was a circle of chairs, a broken-down television with a pile of magazines by the side, and a heap of kid's toys. Everything was decorated in grey and the place looked drab.

In the changing room I saw René, a frail version of her former self. She was standing next to the mirror, topless, looking as if she was on speed. Her breasts had sagged and her face was drawn and tired looking. It had been about a year since I had seen her last, and since then, she told me, she'd had a baby. A condom had broken with a client and she'd got pregnant. She didn't have an abortion because she needed all the money for heroin, and she was still an addict right the way through the birth. I felt sorry for her and the baby, and I couldn't believe that she'd been that badly addicted to smack.

As I was getting dressed, I saw a few of the other girls I'd worked with before. There was Diane, the grandmother with a heart of gold. Tracey was still there, and so were Kylie and another, old Jay, who owned three houses from working. Then there was June, the hilarious Thai girl, and Amanda who was always complaining about something.

I was glad to be back. I could relate to these girls as my friends because they'd been through what I had. They knew what it was like to feel the way you did when you sold your body, and why you did it and why you kept on doing it, even though it fucked you up. Working here always fucked me up, and it looked like it had been fucking everyone else up as well, but we still kept coming back for more.

I think sometimes I could smell the rotting flesh of the place. You could almost sense the neglect and sickness in the air. It was as if this place had become the last stop off from life itself. More girls than ever were using drugs now, and those who had spent years wasting their bodies on smack began to show the emotional strain. I wondered what they would do next. What I was going to do next?

I stayed working there throughout the summer, and instead of being outdoors and in cafes with friends I spent it at work. If I liked making myself miserable, I was doing a good job. I felt at least some comradeship with the girls. We were in it together — sort of.

I know everyone has their hard luck story, and practically all working girls have theirs. I felt sorry for myself, and I saw no justice in life. In fact I saw nothing in life, just days and years to fill in time. Then when I'm dead, that's it, I thought, maybe then I can get some peace.

I wasn't the most positive person alive: in fact my attitude to life was very negative. I didn't hope any more for anything, because when I did it all went wrong. I thought I had been unlucky from the day I was born, and I blamed my brother, my mum, Mark, anyone, for my unhappiness. I wasn't intelligent and I'd lost my looks and health, and I had no money and not enough friends.

I got tired of the long nights at the Meeting Place and I

started working more at home. The clients in brothels were hard to handle; at least when I worked at home, I was better treated. They didn't pull me around or regard me as shit, and I got to keep all the money. The nights I did go to work I would tell the girls about working privately, and how the money was much better. It got back to the owner that I was trying to persuade the girls to work for themselves. It would be bad business if some of the girls left. I had a feeling they had their spies listening to what I was saying to everyone.

I felt better when I worked at home. It wasn't so hard on my body and I got to work in surroundings that I had created, so I felt more comfortable. I advertised first only in the local papers because it was cheaper and I didn't have to spend too much time on the phone, because only so many people would read it. But the response was always good. If I got up early and finished about six, I was guaranteed at least three clients. I was charging them one hundred and fifty for an hour and eighty for half. The clients were middle of the range, mainly nine-to-fivers, and a few had their own businesses. When they buzzed to come up I'd take them straight through to my room, and ask them for the money and then I'd get them to take a shower. If I felt anything was wrong, I'd say that it would be better if they left, and called another time.

Some clients were weird. I remember an accountant I saw who fucked like a wooden toy, and when he couldn't stick it up my arse, he got angry because he thought he could do anything he wanted. I'd dealt with clients like him before, and usually I just told them to leave. I never gave them their money back either.

A few times, when the clients hadn't got what they wanted, they'd get nasty. Usually it had to do with coming twice in half an hour. There was one guy that I saw, who came quickly, in the first five minutes. He'd enquired beforehand on the phone about the prices and had said he couldn't afford an hour, but was half an hour okay. He turned out to be one of those clock watchers, wanting to know before he gave me the money when the time started — before or after his shower.

Lying on the bed naked with him, I tried to give him a massage, as I did with all the clients, but he said, pushing my head down to his cock, that he was here for the sex, not a back-rub. I knew he was going to be a problem and after he'd come and had a five minute rest, he wanted to start all over again. I refused. We argued for the next twenty minutes until his time was up. He got up and dressed, saying it was a lot of money for nothing.

Then there were the brothel bookings you'd have to pull out of because they got too rough. These could turn nasty and you'd have too be careful not to get hurt, although in some cases, depending on the girl, it might be the client who would have to be careful not to get hurt. Some girls would give the money back regardless, but not many, because they knew the receptionist would always back them up.

I worked at the Meeting Place at weekends because I just needed to be there. Even though I was making enough money at my place, I couldn't stop myself from going in. I knew my hair was falling out as a result of being there, and it was at the front this time, where it was hard to cover. But still I kept going in. I was to me like the needle to the junkie needle. Now I understood how girls felt who used drugs — it was a need that had to be filled.

It was around this time I met Brad at the Meeting Place. He came in at the end of the night and asked me straight away whether I did bondage. I said, yes I did. He followed me through to a room, and handed over one hundred dollars and said he had a lot more depending on how things worked out. He was carrying a trendy mobile phone and he looked and sounded as if he was important. He wasn't particularly good-looking and had curly blond hair that was receding at the front.

He said he'd been doing speed, and when I came back into the room, he already had a few lines for me to do. I didn't take speed, especially not at five in the morning when I was just about to go to bed, so I declined the offer.

He snorted up all the lines and lay down on the bed with just his boxer shorts on. I went to get undressed but he said I could leave my clothes on if I preferred. He wanted me to sit on top of him while he masturbated. He struggled to get away and I held him down with my thighs. I was sitting on his chest and leaning over, talking dirty to him. He was quite strong, but it was an easy booking, even though I'd hated the fact that he tried to push speed onto me.

Every time he came in after that, he wanted the same thing. I found him interesting. He was humorous and easy to talk to, and usually I hated talking to clients. He came back for me quite a few times, and another time, when he'd had a big win at the casino, he booked me right through the night, and then asked me whether I wanted to come back to his place for a private booking.

I did, and I was surprised that he was living in a small dumpy flat in Prahran. He'd been telling me that he was an advertising executive and that he was working for a big agency, which was what impressed me about him the most. The studio was for the weekends, he said, so he could have somewhere to smoke dope since his girlfriend was straight, and didn't smoke. I sat down on the sofa and he offered me a pipe and I got stoned like I used to. It really hit me because he'd persuaded me to do a few lines before that, and I felt the full effect of the drugs in my body. I could hardly speak and everything I said came out wrong. I kept apologising for being so dumb and then I thought, he's paying me for my time and I must sound like an idiot. And he was the big advertising executive talking to me. I felt so small. I just lay on the sofa listening to him talk. He was so intelligent and he could talk about anything.

I remember asking him whether he woke up in the morning happy to be alive. It was a deep question for me — even though I was on drugs, I always woke up wondering what the fuck I was going to do and the day gradually got worse from there. I thought maybe I was looking at things the wrong way. He seemed to have a lot of answers to questions about life. His intelligence turned me on even if his looks didn't. He wasn't like the rest of the clients. He was smart; he gave me a different outlook on life.

He always wanted me to do his fantasy, and since he was the one paying, I obliged. He didn't like normal sex. He liked his fantasy. He was a strong person. He would come and see me at the end of the night and was like my knight in shining armour. I felt he was rescuing me from the lecherous clients. I looked forward to him coming in, and I liked his accent and the way he said my name, always sharp and clear. I would get all shy and embarrassed, and I only spoke to him when he wanted to talk to me. He told me he only did it on weekends.

I knew he didn't just come in on weekends, and I thought maybe he was lying about being in advertising as well. He came in on the weekdays to get speed from Tracy or one of the other girls.

He was the one, in the end, who would cure my addiction to the Meeting Place by getting me sacked. It was indirectly his fault, because they thought I was seeing him outside of work and they also knew that I was working privately. But at that stage he wasn't paying me anything. I was just seeing him as a friend. I was shocked at first; I'd never been sacked from a brothel, and I thought it was pretty cool being sacked from the worst brothel in Melbourne.

Now I would have to rely totally on the money I earned privately at home. Brad gave me the idea of working as a high-class hooker, but I didn't feel I had the confidence to pull it off.

Then I met Emma. I saw her ad in the Truth, looking for girls to work with. I called her up and she sounded charming on the phone. I asked her how much she charged for an hour and I was astonished that she asked for two hundred dollars. We arranged to meet for lunch, and I was excited to know what she'd be like. She'd told me she was in her late thirties and she advertised as having the body of a schoolgirl.

Lunch was at a hotel in the city, where she'd just finished a booking. Somehow she didn't look like a prostitute as I introduced myself and took a seat opposite her. She smiled warmly at me from eyes heavy with make-up and lips carefully painted. She wore a blue tailored suit that made her look very business-like, especially when our conversation was interrupted by her mobile phone, which rang constantly with inquiries from potential clients.

Emma told me how she'd worked for over twenty years as a high-class hooker. She had a lot of regulars and not enough time, and now she was slowly trying to get out of working and she wanted someone to take on some of her regulars. She, of course, would take a third of what I made because she got me the booking.

It sounded okay. I wasn't always busy at home, and I could make some extra money from her regulars. She already had a booking for that night, if I wanted, with a gentleman from Sydney who flew down every two weeks to see her. His name was Brian, she told me, and he wanted to share two girls. So that night, outside the hotel where we'd had lunch, Brad dropped me off on the way to the casino, and I sat waiting for her in reception. I watched her as she breezed through the hotel, and her eyes lit up as she saw me. The light was harsher and not so flattering this time, and I noticed the wrinkles and acne scars underneath the heavy make-up. She was dressed in a business suit again, as was I, but I couldn't help thinking we looked like such hookers, still stumbling around the hotel in stilettos at eleven o'clock at night.

Emma's phone started ringing as we waited for the lift, one of her old regulars in town again. I felt myself blushing and I looked away in embarrassment as a group of people pretended not to hear while Emma went on about when she'd be free from this booking, oblivious of the fact that people don't really have great opinions of hookers. I tried to make myself disappear, as a deathly silence took us up to the sixth floor, where Emma and I got out and looked around for the right room number.

Brian, Emma explained, was really nice but he was always stoned when he booked her and that annoyed her. However, he was paying five hundred for the booking, and I would get two hundred of that. I gasped at the thought of getting two hundred dollars for a booking.

As I was to see, the clients changed when the price went up. Brian was more sophisticated than the average client and I watched as Emma made a fuss over him before we got down to business. Emma asked Brian whether he was happy with her discovery — meaning me — and he beamed at me as I stood there in all my nakedness, ready for action.

I looked at Emma's naked body, that was well-proportioned for her height. She was only five foot but she had pert breasts and a toned and taut body. Her blonde hair had been cut to a bob and she had a warm smile, but she wasn't particularly good-looking. What made Emma was her sophisticated attitude and the ability and confidence to ask for so much money.

But for that price she did oral without a condom and towards the end of the booking, when Brian was in between us, lying on his side sucking my nipples, Emma was on his other side with her fingers up his arse. I didn't see her put a glove on, and as soon as the booking was over, she got up straight away to wash her hands, and to bring Brian a warm towel to mop up his come. Obviously she was quite intimate with her regulars, and I thought to myself, for that price I would probably have to be intimate in some way too.

Emma handed me the money on the way to the lift, while she was already taking another call from a client. She'd left her mobile on during the booking and to Brian's and my amusement, she was answering calls right in the middle of things. I left her as she waved me goodbye at the lobby and, just before I was about to go, she reached for me and hugged me affectionately. I had a feeling that Emma was lonely just like me.

Now I'd seen a high-class hooker in action I put it into practice myself. The only thing that made a high-class hooker high was the money she asked for and the attitude. It didn't really have much to do with looks, but charm and how well you dressed came into it.

Amazingly, after about ten enquiries a client agreed to book me. It was the same as any other booking I did, except I gave oral without a condom, and politely asked for the money at the end of the booking, while I hitched up my new designer skirt. I started to take their names and numbers to call them back so I knew they weren't just wasting my time. They'd come over to my place and I'd try and make it look as neat and expensive as possible. In these surroundings I really felt I was over-charging but I was quite a bit younger than Emma, so I hoped that would make up for it.

The Prostitution Trap

After a few days, I dropped the price to a hundred and seventy, and one hundred and twenty for half an hour, because I hated giving the clients oral without a condom, and I didn't think the money was worth the risk. I rang up Emma and told her I was busy with my own clients and I didn't need the extra ones. She sounded annoyed and I suppose I would have been too in her place.

I decided to move out from South Yarra: now I was turning my home into a proper business I needed more space and a nicer flat. Brad gave me the idea of living in East Melbourne. He joked that that's where high-class hookers would probably live. I found a two-bedroom apartment that was twice the size of my other flat and, with an extra bedroom, it gave me more space in which to put all my belongings, so I didn't have all the clients going through them.

As soon as I moved in I went full out on advertising in every newspaper I could. My phone rang hot and I was non-stop busy for weeks. I'd promised myself this time I would work for one more year, save as much money as I could, and then stop and start another business. I wasn't sure what type of business but I had some sort of business in mind. Brad was the one giving me the motivation to make a lot of money.

While I was in South Yarra a client had given me the idea of writing a book about being a prostitute. I thought it was a good idea, because I'd always thought the books and articles I'd read on prostitution made it sound glamorous and exciting, when really it was nothing like that at all.

I remember reading an article in a women's magazine, a diary of a prostitute and what it said was ridiculous. It was as if a local pimp had paid for the story to be printed to encourage new girls to work: everything they said was the complete opposite to how it really was.

The reality of it is that it's a hard and lonely road, and you can't lead a normal life while you're doing it. First there's the secrecy. You can't tell anyone what you're doing, so you isolate yourself, or lie. I'd done both and neither had worked out. You feel you're not real. You can't have decent boyfriends because there are not many men who will respect you for what you do. I knew of some girls who'd got lucky with husbands and boyfriends who didn't mind, but they were usually the ones who were pimping from them.

Even though I had a good business going and I was making about three thousand a week, it was an incredible strain on my health. A lot of it would have been caused by just the thought of sleeping with so many men. I was seeing about five clients a day and I was hardly ever turned on. It was just like a job. And the hard part was having to entertain them, relax them and then get them off. I know I was used to it, but saying hi to a stranger, and then both taking your clothes off and having sex was not all that easy.

Clients were never that good-looking; after all they were paying for what they wanted. About one in fifty would be sexy naked, but the rest had pot bellies, wrinkly skin, saggy balls, fat arses, hair just about everywhere, bad breath — in fact just about everything you would find unattractive. Quite a few were married or in a relationship. The majority of the singles were too wrapped up in their business or work to have time for a girl.

I built up a steady flow of regulars who would visit me weekly. They varied greatly and so did what they wanted. They'd improved from the clients I used to see in South Yarra, and some of them actually cared about me. My favourites were the ones who just wanted to keep it simple. I'd gone off fantasies and now preferred straight sex. But I still had the guys who wanted the schoolgirl fantasy — it seemed no matter where I went, they still found me.

Mike was a regular who liked me to act like a young girl. He would spank my arse quite hard and push my head down to suck his cock. He was about sixty, very well-mannered. At the end of the booking he liked to fuck me face down so he could ram his cock really hard into me, as if he was raping me. I would moan softly like a young girl, and he'd come for ages. He made me sick and I hated him, but the booking only went for about twenty minutes, and he paid me one hundred and seventy dollars for that.

My worst client was Victor. He was a dirty, filthy truckie who'd followed me from my old place at South Yarra. I hated seeing him, and he still only paid my old prices, too. He was fat and ugly and he stank so badly it was sickening, and he was always on some pills to keep him going. Even after he'd had a shower he still stank and I had to block my nose while I sucked his cock. The smell would go through the condom and he would push my head into his groin telling me 'to suck it babe'. He'd jump around the room telling me to suck his cock, and only when he was sure my mouth couldn't suck any more would he tell me to stop and hop on top so he could blow. It was like sitting on a huge mountain of junk food. He was living, breathing proof that you are what you eat. But because I knew him it was easier than seeing a stranger, and it was a regular ninety dollars into my pocket and into my savings. The thought of seeing him now would send me running in the opposite direction with a can of air freshener. I did anything for money back then.

I saw a famous heart surgeon who'd flown in from overseas to do an operation that was written up in the paper. I thought he was charming and easy to do when I first saw him, but when I saw him another time he asked me whether I would mind doing a wrestling fantasy. He'd been fine before so I couldn't see a problem, and he was going to pay me two hundred dollars.

In my lounge-room I spread a sheet on the floor and he left me a pair of wrestlers' boots and jocks to get changed into, while he went to get changed in my bedroom. Besides the boots and jocks, I was naked and when he came out he rubbed baby oil into my body and then into his. Then we started to wrestle. I'd expected playful fighting but without warning he grabbed me by the neck and tried to pull me down to the ground by force. He was really hurting and the baby oil made it harder to grip, and caused more pain. I was pissed off so I tripped him over and sent him flying down on his back. He got up again and lunged at me, and I went flying against the couch. He was lying against me, breathing hard, and he looked up and smiled and said, 'I've come'.

I'd been misled into believing he wasn't going to hurt me but what was the point in arguing then. It had only taken ten minutes and we'd finished. He asked for some of his money back but, after that much pain, there was no way he was getting anything. After he left I tried to massage the muscles he'd pulled in my neck and lay down with a blinding headache, crying.

A client I saw one day when I hadn't been getting many calls said over the phone that he wanted a fantasy of some sort, but he didn't know quite what. When he got over, he was a cheerful, plump man in his late twenties, who was running a chain of restaurants. It looked as if he might have splurged on a few drugs that afternoon, judging by the amount of energy he had. He said he was so horny, and he wanted me to dress up in lingerie. I pranced about the room in provocative poses, sticking my arse up in the air and pulling my pants down and showing him my pussy.

He wanted to see me take a piss in the toilet and even though I'd done so many golden showers before, I'd never actually let a client watch me on the toilet. He said, just pretend then, so I did, and that turned the entire booking around. Whether he knew it before, or he'd just discovered it, he was a real piss-drinker. He wanted to see me piss standing up while he lay on the floor masturbating with towels everywhere, and then he wanted me to piss in his mouth, over his cock, everywhere. It went for hours. He wanted to carry right on into the night but five hours of pissing and prancing around had exhausted me, and I'd had enough. He paid me a stack of money for my time and said I was a great girl and left. I never knew piss could be worth so much.

Answering calls from clients all day long really got to me after a while. I know some girls would go about their daily business taking calls wherever they were, but I was very self-conscious about people knowing what I did. I know that it is the oldest profession in the world, but there is no way I'd stand in a queue at the supermarket, or sit in a restaurant, telling a client what I'd do for money.

So I'd sit at home all day answering calls, or not work. I got tired of sitting around so I started reading in between clients. I dug up the old Superlearning book I'd found in Sydney in a new Superlearning 2000 format. I bought it and read it from cover to cover in one week and decided my brain needed a big boost. In it they said that accelerated learning to special Superlearning music could bring out the 91 per cent of the brain we don't normally use. Anything that could make me more intelligent than I was had to be good. I sent off to New York for the tapes and hoped there was a genius lurking inside my head.

Chapter 12

Free

Brad was still on the scene. I'd been seeing him weekends and going over to his place. He'd told me that he'd stopped taking so much speed and was now only smoking bongs. He'd moved from the flat he'd been using at weekends to a nicer house in Richmond, explaining that his girlfriend was now overseas in England and he'd be joining her later on in the year.

I'd grown fond of Brad; I liked him more as friend, and someone to confide in, than anything else. He liked listening about my clients and when I told him about Jordan he seemed to understand. He still liked doing his fantasy and he'd usually have two or three bongs before we did it. He'd stopped offering bongs to me because he preferred girls not to smoke. I resented the fact that he got stoned and I didn't, but I was a tangled up mess of emotions, so I just took out my frustrations in being a perfect sucker.

Brad was always calling me up on my mobile when I was answering calls. He'd say he was with a client at work closing up an account with a few ideas he'd had for an ad. His job sounded so exciting and glamorous and he'd always agree with me when I said he was lucky. He'd told me his parents were both architects, and they'd left Russia when he was twelve to escape the communist system. His family had since done very well in Australia and had a very successful business. Brad was their only child and, after studying law at university, he had gone on to be a successful tennis player in America. I was very impressed with his background and at times I was envious of him. I'd always wanted to be in advertising and he always seemed to be having fun.

By spring I'd worn myself out. I'd been seeing clients non-stop, but I was a long way from reaching the goal of saving the amount of money I had in mind. I was making a lot of money but I also had rent to pay, bills, my mobile phone and advertising costs, and it seemed the harder I tried the harder it became. I started neglecting my health by not eating and allowing myself to become stressed over clients. I let it get to the stage where I came down with a bad case of tonsillitis and ended up in hospital. They just took one look at my tonsils, connected me to a drip and started pumping penicillin into my body before I choked.

I went home three days later, feeling a little better but still very sick. I wished I had family to look after me. Brad drove me back home, dropped me off and said he'd call me the next day. The medication I had to take was giving me the most terrifying nightmares, so here I was still desperately sick, trapped in my dreams and going through hell.

After I recovered, I was very weak, and I thought I'd better slow down and stop seeing so many clients. Brad started coming over more during the week, not just at the weekend. We'd go out to dinner together or to the movies and he'd stay over at my place, or I at his. He still liked me on top of him, doing his fantasy. I guess everyone wants something.

I started smoking bongs with him. At first he hated the fact that I was smoking his dope. He always said that you should be able to take care of yourself and not take from others. It was only dope, I said.

I was still pretty pathetic when I was stoned. I would become disorientated and panicky. But smoking did slow me down. By the time I'd got up, had breakfast with Brad before he left, and got ready myself, it was already one in the afternoon. Before this pattern set in, the alarm would wake me at nine o'clock, I'd jog around the park for half an hour, quickly shower and put on make-up and start answering calls, at the same time as I was making breakfast for clients who liked to have a quickie before work. Now my bookings were going down and I was earning less money, but I was also less stressed.

Brad started leaving me dope to smoke when he wasn't there. He said it would make me sleep better. I got used to smoking more and being a little more lazy. Smoking dope made me think of Brad a lot when he wasn't there. After one bong I was gone. Sometimes it had a bad effect on me and I'd have to calm myself down, but other times I would be fine. I'd just watch television and laugh at whatever was going on.

Spring passed in to summer and before I knew it Christmas was nearly around again. Brad wanted to go on a holiday with me to Noosa; he had a friend up there who wanted to talk about going into business together. I didn't have any plans for Christmas, other than staying alone in my apartment, so I agreed to go.

That was a mistake, agreeing to go on a holiday with Brad. From the moment he booked the flight at the last minute, till we left at six in the morning, I knew I was doing the wrong thing. He was irritated for no reason at all, and as soon as we landed in Noosa, before we even made it to our apartment, he drove straight round to a dealer's place to score some dope. He was abusive to me and aggressive to everyone except his dope dealer.

We drove down to the resort he'd booked us into, which turned out to be only half-built, and our apartment was on the main road. It could have been a nightmare, but I knew only too well I was the one who had agreed to this. He'd paid for everything so I could hardly complain — but I did.

After one night of what felt like sleeping in the middle of the road, and having terrible nightmares, I told him I wanted somewhere better to stay — and I'd pay half this time. We went flat hunting for a beach-side apartment, and I fell in love with a place decorated in blue, with space outside for a barbecue and loungers with a perfect view of the ocean. It was ideal.

We went back to the resort and started packing. While all this was happening he'd arranged to meet his friends an hour later for a day out on their yacht. I knew only too well from experience back home that Brad had no concept of time.

Brad was irritable and impatient and, when he had problems getting a refund from the manager, lost his temper. He lost it so badly that the manager's wife feared for her husband's safety and called the police, unbeknown to Brad. I came out of the apartment having finished packing to find him struggling with the police, with blood all over his face. He shouted at me to call one of his friends, but I had had enough. As the police were taking him away, I went over to him and told him I never wanted to see him again, he was too much. I was flying back to Melbourne without him, out of this nightmare.

I didn't feel guilty about leaving him there — he'd lied to me and taken me there under false pretence. He'd said we'd be staying in a nice apartment, not some half-built resort in the middle of a busy highway, and we were meant to be here to have some fun and relax, and it had been anything but that. I was supposed to be his friend and he'd taken me along as his whore, expecting me to perform his fantasy. Seeing how violent Brad had been had really frightened me; it made me remember what I'd been through with Jordan. I re-booked my flight making my mind up never to see Brad again. My instincts told me something was wrong. It had been a dramatic few days. Coming into Melbourne was a relief, to know that I was away from Brad and what had happened had given me a good excuse to end our relationship.

Christmas was lonely. I was back in my apartment with only my thoughts for company. I started to really think about life and what it had come to, to spend the fourth Christmas in a row alone. On Christmas Day I read a book called Freedom from Sexual Abuse. It inspired me and made me think about giving up work. I wondered how much my past was playing itself out in my life now. Ever since I'd been working it felt as if I was abusing my body, but it didn't really matter because money was the big compensation for all the hurt I'd been through. I was so miserable: there had to be something wrong somewhere.

Brad called on Boxing Day to apologise and, like a fool, I believed everything he said, including the promise that he wasn't going to smoke dope any more and that he was going to keep his temper under control. His parents were paying his fines and he was flying back the next day. He'd spent the last five days, over the Christmas period in jail.

My Christmas was ruined, spent inside my apartment and I was in no party mood. In fact I had begun to wonder where my life was really heading. I didn't feel like working any more. If I worked I would feel worse, and it seemed that at last I was beginning to realise the vicious cycle I was in.

Brad came back from Queensland and we made up. Everything seemed fine and I thought we'd forgiven each other until we slept together that night. I'd missed him and I was more passionate than usual, but my vagina became swollen from the force he used with his fingers. Maybe in his own sick way he was getting back at me. But even the throbbing pain was better than being alone.

I told him how I wanted to give up work and stop tor-

turing myself. I told him that I wanted to look for a normal job and lead a normal life. I was sick and tired of seeing clients who didn't care, of answering the phone to
anyone and then taking the risks. I was tired of abusing
my body and putting myself through so much pain. I'd
lost count of the number of times I'd been hurt by clients.
I thought about writing and working on my book, but I
needed a job to do that. I'd always liked writing so I thought
maybe I could make some money writing ads; after all
that's what Brad did.

I went to check out the career courses at RMIT, and
found the real name for writing ads was copywriting. I discovered there was an AWARD School of copywriting, which
ran a competition each year to help writers get into advertising. I thought about entering it; I had nothing to lose.
I'd found out more about advertising in the last two hours
than I had from Brad in the last eight months. I even began to wonder whether Brad really was in advertising.

I carried on writing my book in the day-time, in between telling myself that I had to go and look for a job
soon, and somewhere less expensive to live. Brad had told
me to relax and take my time, there was no rush, jobs and
accommodation were't going to run away from me. So I
did. I had enough money saved and Brad said he'd help
me pay my rent.

He'd been paying for a lot of things just recently, like
dinner, and he'd been giving me money here and there.
He'd even bought me a new phone. I was grateful for his
help, and I tried to forget about what had happened before. He would come over to my place in the afternoon
while I was writing and sometimes we'd have sex, but it

wasn't like the sex we'd had before; it had changed since he'd come back from Queensland. Even though I never realised it, Brad must have guessed all along that I liked submissive sex. I felt so much more, and it was so much easier for me to come if he rammed his fingers hard into my cunt, or sucked really hard on my breasts and then fucked me inside, hard and deep. The first time he did it I was angry, because he'd done it without asking, but now I wanted him to hurt me; I wanted his finger up my arse and his cock thrusting inside my vagina, making it swollen and sore. And while he was doing it, I'd think about the abuse I had gone through when I was young, and I'd imagine my brother sticking his fingers inside me and his friends joining in while I was sitting on top fucking Brad's cock.

The more submissive sex I did, the more it made me think about the abuse I'd been through. I remembered back when I was five, sitting in the long grass in next-door's garden, with my pants down, and my brother telling his friend to take a piss inside me —I remembered the panic that spread through my body, and then left when he didn't do it. I remembered the time hidden behind the cars in a car park, sitting on my neighbour's knee — he was about eighteen, and he'd be feeling my cunt — along with my brother and his friend.

I think because I was still smoking dope it made things look worse. I wondered just how far I would let Brad go; maybe I'd let him use a knife. If I wanted him to inflict that much pain on me how would I know when to stop? Would he know when to stop?

But at the same time I began reading books about child

abuse and studying Superlearning. This gave me new ways of looking at life. I tried to let go of the past and to forgive my abusive brother and his friends and let bygones be by-gones.

I'd become more aware from studying Superlearning and I started living in the here and now, and really felt more alive. It was as if I had been welcomed back to the land of the living. Strange events began to happen when I let go of all the pain and hate I had felt before, and started to love.

I started to love Brad, not because he was the closest thing to me, but because it was better for me to love and stop living in a world of hate and revenge. I began to feel lighter and more relaxed. It was if my life had become more meaningful and exciting. I felt in touch with God, and I'd never been a great believer before. Somehow because I'd connected with the universe and nature and spirituality, and had started to believe in greater forces, the more trivial side of life no longer bothered me as much.

I think the relaxation techniques I'd been doing with Superlearning had a good effect on me. Stress-free learning fine-tuned my mind, enabling me to tap into some of that hidden potential I'd read about. It was as if a tidal wave of learning had swept me up and drenched my mind, not just with knowledge, but with a more intuitive, har-monious sense of being.

I'd also been reading self-help books on the effects of child abuse and they had a strong effect on me as well. And the more tolerant and caring I became towards Brad, the less annoyed and stressed out I was. But Brad wasn't stupid; he knew he had a lot of control over my life.

But things didn't stay that way. The longer I put off finding a job, the worse I thought my chances would be. Smoking at night-time was making me lazier and Brad continued to pay my rent and give me money from time to time. As time wore on, I began to sleep with him less and less and became less motivated in finding a job because I had somewhere to live, paid for, I was getting money from him and now I didn't even have to fuck him very often.

I still had alopecia and I began to worry constantly about what was going to happen, and even though I felt a thousand times better now I'd given up work, I still felt that something was wrong.

There was a gay dance party coming up. I'd been to one at New Year with Brad, but as usual, everything I did with Brad turned out exactly the opposite of what I hoped for. He'd ruined that party and my New Year, but he promised that we'd go to this party and that everything would be okay. I accepted this because I was relying on him more and more for everything — money, rent, drugs and so on.

The night before the party, he brought over some speed and said he wanted to do a few lines, and afterwards I took my clothes off and went through his fantasy the way I used to when I met him at the Meeting Place.

Although I had been determined to love Brad, the longer the relationship went on and the more drugs we did together, gradually made me see him in a different light. It was hard to be loving and tolerant on speed; instead I became irritable and intolerant and a little bit frightened, as I realised that he was trying to manipulate me. I hated the fact that he prevented me from doing things, and I hated myself for being so complacent around him. I also hated the fact that he was so possessive of my every minute and my every action.

Next day, after shopping for clothes and picking up the dance tickets, I went back home in a good mood, pleased that I had managed to get myself together. Brad said he would pay for the evening so I needn't draw any money from my own account. But it transpired that this was only so I wouldn't have any money for the dance party. I had a feeling he didn't even want me to go, but why didn't he just say so, instead of sneaking around trying to control my life. I had a little bit of money left over from shopping; enough for drinks anyway.

We snorted up what was left of the drugs and Brad encouraged me to have a few bongs. My body was going up and down and my mind swirling from high to low. I felt panicky, worn out and run down. Brad was smoking so much dope that I couldn't believe he could feel okay, but he just kept going. I knew I'd taken way too much, in fact I'd never taken so much speed two days in a row with no sleep in between. My instincts were telling me something was wrong, but nowadays I never knew whether I was over-reacting or not. In the last few weeks since I'd stopped hating Brad for what he did, mysterious things were happening that I couldn't even begin to explain. I didn't know whether it was real or not, but whenever I tried to fill my heart with love instead of hate I could feel a spiritual force helping me somehow.

But now I felt frightened. It was as if Brad had some ulterior motive. We got to the dance party and I was glad to get away from my flat and conversation with Brad. I felt lighter and safer knowing there were hundreds of people around me, after being confined to the company of one person for the last two days.

Brad looked miserable, probably because he felt uncomfortable being at a gay dance party. We'd only been there about an hour and he already wanted to go home. I, on the other hand, even though I was tired and coming down from drugs, wanted to stay. Brad didn't want to go without me, but finally he left.

I watched him walk out, back down the driveway to the car park, and I felt relieved that I'd finally got rid of him — he'd been driving me crazy. I walked back inside, alone, but exhilarated, not really knowing what to expect.

This party was more gay than New Year's Eve, and I felt I was dressed for the part in knee-high boots, a short skirt and a yellow singlet top with no bra underneath. Brad had hated it and I knew the words 'dirty' and 'slut' had been going through his head.

I had a strange feeling that something was going to happen. A fair was all laid out outside the shed, with rides and stalls — it gave the party a really different atmosphere. I wanted to be close to the dance floor and the pounding music, so I got a drink with the money I had left, and walked back through the crowd of dancers. As I was passing through, a dancer with long hair stopped me. He asked me my name as we started dancing and said I had the same name as his last girlfriend. As we went on talking, he seemed to realise that I was quite distressed. I asked him if he had any speed or E, and told him briefly about Brad. He asked whether I wanted to talk about it outside.

Leaning up against the railings by the water, I poured my heart out to this stranger I'd met just five minutes before. I told him that I used to work as a prostitute and that I'd recently stopped, but my boyfriend was making me feel trapped and frightened, that I was scared he was going to do something crazy. I went on to tell him how he'd been giving me dope to smoke every night and how he'd been helping me financially. I also told him that I'd become frightened about having submissive sex and that Brad was the one who always initiated it. My life revolved around him and I didn't have a job or much security of my own.

What this stranger told me next made more sense than I'd been making for the last two months. He told me that I hadn't stopped working; I was still working as a hooker for my boyfriend. I was his private whore. He was paying my rent, he'd been giving me dope to smoke every night to keep me tired and destroy my motivation to find a job and he had me right where he wanted me, isolated in a flat, tucked away for him to come round and fuck.

But all I ever wanted to do was to love him, I said, realisation now dawning on me that I had unknowingly become Brad's whore. Surely I was free to love anyone; I could love the world, I didn't just have to love him. But right now I belonged to him. I was beginning to understand.

I heard the music stop inside the shed and watched girls dressed up like prostitutes strut their stuff on stage. I put my arms around my stranger and hugged him for understanding and trying to make me understand too. Everyone rushed outside as fireworks lit up the sky in the distance. I felt my tears fall as a surge of relief went through me.

Something was going on, something strange and mysterious. What was it about this party and this stranger I'd just met, who was telling me that he'd had a possessive girlfriend, and about my boyfriend who'd made me into his whore? Here at a gay dance party that stood for personal and sexual freedom.

I was learning something at this party about being whole, about being one, and it was taking on almost a religious light. Somehow I didn't feel impure anymore. I no longer felt like a second-class citizen because I'd been a prostitute, but new and free. Brad seemed a million miles away and he no longer had me in his grip; he was a parasite who had tried to suck my life away.

Now I understood what my instincts were telling me as I took my stranger and went to the side of the dance floor. We started to kiss and touch each other. It felt good to be free and to be doing what I wanted.

We went outside and had sex on one of the trailers. As we fucked, and I felt his huge cock inside me, I felt relief that he didn't own me, that I was free to have sex with him and enjoy it.

I couldn't get Brad off my mind and I knew the sooner I faced him the better. So I told my stranger I had to go home and sort things out. I gave him my silky gold pants as a memento. I'd memorised his number but I had a feeling I wouldn't call him. Before I left he told me to be careful and only take drugs at dance parties, to stop smoking dope and always use condoms. He warned me about my boyfriend and told me not to say anything about what had happened tonight. I kissed him goodbye and, walking back to the gate, took one last glance at him before I left the party on a natural high and with a strong feeling that my life was going to change for the better.

When I got back home I was almost too scared to go inside my own flat. Brad was sitting on the couch, stoned, with sleeping pills spread all over the table. The lounge-room had taken on a strange and different light and the air tasted of death. I sat down next to Brad and drank in the dark atmosphere. Now I saw him in his true light I realised how he'd slithered into my life. Well he could slither out again.

I asked him to leave and take his clothes and everything else, to just go. I didn't want him in my life anymore and he knew if I wanted to close the door and lock him out of my life, then there wasn't much he could do about it, except to bide his time and try to crawl back in. He looked at me and snarled that I was unstable but he was going anyway. He said I'd better not contact him or else, and glared at me.

Suddenly the phone rang — it was my mum. She was calling from England to see how I was. I tried to stay as calm as possible, and tell her everything was okay. Brad looked on amazed. Of all the times she could have called, she'd called now.

After he'd packed everything into his car, he came back for one last cigarette. The atmosphere in the room was eerie as he sat on the couch next to the revolving fan. I watched the fan turn around and around. It reminded me of one of the rides I'd seen at the dance party. Brad emptied the remaining sleeping pills onto the table and said they were just like smoking dope. It was as if he was trying to draw me into his world of drugs one last time.

I didn't argue; I just let him say his piece before he left. He was living in a differerent world from mine now, a world that looked dark and was full of drugs and lies. It was really so obvious. He was like bad karma; he was like that fan swirling around. Because I'd been living in my own dark world I'd attracted someone like him. Only when I'd started to give up taking revenge on him had something happened to open my eyes to a new way.

We said our goodbyes on the stairs and I told him to be strong. I told him I'd be his friend if he wanted, but only because I couldn't help feeling something for him. And then he disappeared into the bad karma wasteland and drugs fantasy that he'd come from, out of my life for good.

Epilogue

I changed after that. I finally gave up bruising my soul once and for all.

I never heard from Brad again, although I heard from his friends that he'd lied about himself, even about the work he did!

I left him in my past. I found a new place to live in a different area and became a complete person at last, with a new outlook on life. I got into the AWARD school of copywriting and started doing something I really enjoyed.

Realising I'd learnt something from all those years of working as a prostitute, I decided to finish my book: I felt it had something to say about prostitution — the real unglamorised version of sex for money — and the reality of freedom for the sexes.